THE XINGYI BOXING MANUAL

THE XINGYI BOXING MANUAL

REVISED AND EXPANDED EDITION

EDITED BY Jin Yunting
COMPILED BY Ling Guiqing
TRANSLATED BY John Groschwitz

BLUE SNAKE BOOKS
BERKELEY, CALIFORNIA

Published by Blue Snake Books, an imprint of North Atlantic Books
P.O. Box 12327
Berkeley, California 94712

Cover and book design by Susan Quasha
Printed in the United States of America

The Xingyi Boxing Manual: Revised and Expanded Edition is sponsored and published by the Society for the Study of Native Arts and Sciences (dba North Atlantic Books), an educational nonprofit based in Berkeley, California, that collaborates with partners to develop cross-cultural perspectives, nurture holistic views of art, science, the humanities, and healing, and seed personal and global transformation by publishing work on the relationship of body, spirit, and nature.

North Atlantic Books' publications are available through most bookstores. For further information, call 800-733-3000 or visit our websites at www.northatlanticbooks.com and www.bluesnakebooks.com.

Library of Congress Cataloging-in-Publication Data
  [Xing yi quan pu wu gang qi yan lun. English.]
The Xingyi boxing manual / edited by Jin Yunting, compiled by Ling Guiqing, translated by John Groschwitz.—Revised and Expanded Edition.
    pages cm
  Complete title of previous edition: The Xingyi boxing manual : Hebei style's five principles and seven words.
  Includes bibliographical references.
  ISBN 978–1-58394–853–8 (Trade Paper)—ISBN 978–1-58394–854–5 (Ebook)
  1. Hand-to-hand fighting, Oriental. 2. Martial arts—China. I. Jin, Yunting. II. Ling, Guiqing. III. Groschwitz, John.
  GV1112.X5613 2015
  796.815'5—dc23

                            2014030038

1 2 3 4 5 6 7 8 9 UNITED 19 18 17 16 15

Printed on recycled paper

CONTENTS

Calligraphy from the 1931 edition. It reads (R to L):
Mid-autumn, guihai year [1923],
"Skill approaching the Dao"
Sheng Siyi of Wujin

Calligraphy from the 1931 edition. It reads (R to L):
[To] the great athlete Yunting
"The path to health"
Sheng Shengyi

Photo of compiler Ling Guiqing
From the 1930 edition

雲亭先生四十三小象

癸亥仲夏嘉定金砭史頤

Photo of Jin Yunting at age forty-three
Calligraphy by Jin Bianshi of Jiading
The fifth month, guihai year [1923]

無事之家不知其福也
事至始知無事之福矣
無病之身不知其樂也
病生始知無病之樂矣

Calligraphy from the 1931 edition. It reads:

The person without troubles does not recognize their prosperity;
When troubles arrive, then one begins to know the prosperity of being worry-free.
The body without sickness does not recognize its happiness;
When sickness arises, then one begins to know the happiness of being healthy.

Translator's Preface

IT HAS BEEN ROUGHLY a decade since publication of *The Xingyi Boxing Manual: Hebei Style's Five Principles and Seven Words*. At the time, the simple and elegant format of that slim volume—containing the basic "songs" of Xingyi's postures, the images and concepts associated with each element, and the guidelines for practice contained in the "seven words"— seemed like an obvious and essential choice for translation into English. Only several years later did I discover that this short book, published in 1931, was itself an excerpted version of *A Pictorial Explanation of Xingyi Five Element Boxing*, published one year earlier in 1930. This earlier, longer version contained almost all of the material in the 1931 edition, but also offered more detailed discussions of theory, and step-by-step instructions for performing the five elements, accompanied by numerous photos and line drawings. Despite having received widespread attention in Asia—it has been reprinted at least nine times by various presses in Taiwan, Hong Kong, and mainland China—the 1930 edition had yet to be rendered into English, and seemed even more deserving of widespread dissemination. Now, after a long interval, the English-speaking audience finally has the chance to enjoy this unique work.

The *Pictorial Explanation of Xingyi Five Element Boxing* is unique in several ways. First, it comes from a student of both Shang Yunxiang and Sun Lutang, themselves students of Li Cunyi and Guo Yunshen, respectively. This work then is certainly a distillation of the knowledge and experience of several of the major figures in the history of Xingyi boxing and, as such, deserves further study and contemplation. Second, it was born during the Qing/Republican Era transition when martial arts writings were undergoing a renaissance. From the theory section we learn that Jin Yunting and Li Jianqiu both moved south in the first year of the republic (1911–12), and from Wu Shulan's foreword we see that Jin came to Shanghai in 1919. Ling

Guiqing, who was in Shanghai, claims to have compiled the text for Jin, and many of the forewords and calligraphy are dated 1923, implying that the text was compiled sometime during a roughly twelve-year period, and probably in the latter five years, a few years after Sun Lutang's own *Study of Xingyiquan* was published, and contemporaneous with Li Jianqiu's *The Art of Xingyiquan,* published in 1920. Thus, from a comparative standpoint it offers much to broaden our understanding of the art of Xingyiquan at that time. Third, despite the notable martial arts lineage and Jin's obvious social and political connections (he lived at the residence of Sheng Xuanhuai, Minister of Transportation under the Qing and head of the Imperial Bank of China), we can determine little information about him, aside from what is in his biography herein. This translation helps to record the efforts of an obviously active and skilled practitioner, and may perhaps spur others to uncover more about Jin's own subsequent lineage.

This revised and expanded edition of *The Xingyi Boxing Manual* contains all of the material from both the 1930 and 1931 editions, along with the biographies of masters added to the first English edition. Mistakes from the first English edition have been corrected—as have a few mistakes in the original Chinese—and the two editions have been combined with an eye to readability. Where necessary, minor edits of the source text have been made to enhance clarity of explanation. Notes are provided as needed to clarify a specific point, though I have sought to keep these to a minimum. All terms in the book are romanized according to the Pinyin system, and all Chinese names are written according to the Chinese system, i.e., last name first, with characters for the names of Xingyi practitioners following their first occurrence in the text. Certain terms, mostly related to Chinese medicine, have been left in Chinese for clarity's sake, with accompanying references.

The material in this book represents the essential aspects of Xingyi practice as developed and refined over generations and, while not a substitute for a good teacher, it is an essential adjunct to any serious study of this art. As Cui Heqing states in his foreword: "When drinking water, one should ponder its source." We should consider what is contained in these few pages and attempt to understand and analyze its meaning. The more clearly we can understand the classic texts, comparing their alternate versions and styles, the more easily we will be able to seek the subtleties of this profound art. It is my hope that this translation allows the true intent of *The Xingyi Boxing Manual* to be readily understood by the general Xingyi practitioner, and that it furthers the understanding of this art's martial and healing aspects. I have done my utmost to translate these passages faithfully, clearly, and according to their original meaning. Any mistakes contained herein are entirely my own, and I welcome any comments or corrections.

John Groschwitz
Menlo Park, California
New Year's Day 2014

Foreword by Vincent Black

I HAD BEEN LAID up for eight weeks with an internal bleeding injury acquired in training with an effectively inappropriate training partner. I spent those eight weeks recuperating and researching everything I could to find an art that offered effective self-defense capabilities but structured so that I could benefit from the training without the need for a reliable training partner most of the time. When I was on my feet again, I went in search of a Xingyi instructor. Five years later I was teaching Xingyi and have continued for the last thirty-seven years. It is with this hindsight perspective that I can speak with some anecdotal authority and wholeheartedly endorse and affirm the veracity of those earlier testimonies by Master Jin's direct students regarding the profound and distinctive benefits from embracing this art to pursue physical cultivation. Aside from my own recoveries through training, I have witnessed similar occurrences many times with students over the past thirty-seven years.

My professional career as a Doctor of Oriental Medicine, a direct influence of my first Xingyi master, Hsu Hong-Chi, over the years afforded me countless opportunities on a daily basis to observe the "method" at work and to come to more deeply appreciate the excellence of its "science." I can say that the common acknowledgment of Xingyi's ability to produce profound constitutional benefits that in the end "exceed expectations" is in the long view empirically validated and its promised benefits can be relied upon by the enthusiast.

One cannot help but notice the thread of decency that runs common through all the writings of these practitioners, which is an expression of the esteem they hold for each other. This is also associated with our practice. The necessity of martial ethics being considered an essential aspect in any interaction between practitioners is a matter of legend as well as historical fact: from the legendary founder Yue Fei to the historical hero Ji Jike and on through the next few centuries, Xingyi boxers arose in their times to set the moral post upright. The standard for moral ethics and martial virtue is expressed in the phrase "gentleman of heavenly calm and composure," which connotes a cultivated human being. It was considered equally important that one not only did well in achievement, but also equally as well in self-restraint and aversion to temptation of virtues. This has been one of the most attractive and gratifying aspects of my work over the last four decades.

The very nature of Xingyi training is more inwardly oriented than most other martial methods, employing emphatic focus on breathing, prolonged static postures, and quick, adroit movements while in balance to produce smooth, effortless power. The mystery of this "balance" is explained in minute detail in several sections of the book, including the Essential Teachings on Yue Wumu's Xingyiquan. These discussions necessarily interweave the principles of classical Chinese cosmology and Chinese medical theory and simultaneously infuse them into the boxing methodology itself. This speaks strongly to the holistic nature of the art that sets it apart from the plethora of the other available martial arts.

Master Jin was a master teacher, long in experience and understanding, as evinced in his tendency at the end of a long, detailed discussion to close with some wise caveat that addresses typical pitfalls in training that are common to all acolytes due to basic human nature. In his explanation of the nine essential teachings he provides an overall construct of the method itself, which serves to "decode" abstruse or sublime concepts and subsequently sheds new light on and further clarifies images or meanings of other Xingyi sayings or mottoes. Mr. Groschwitz has produced a wonderful contribution for those of us who passionately pursue the art but cannot speak Chinese. Master Jin has afforded us all an opportunity to peer more deeply into the internal experience through his comprehensive detailing of the process from multiple perspectives. I have been working with Mr. Groschwitz and many senior masters of Xingyi for twenty years and watching this work in progress for the last ten years and I see that through his prodigious efforts this edition of *The Xingyi Boxing Manual* is a milestone contribution that will revive anew the propagation of an ancient art that is not necessarily an easy fit in this fast-paced, action-filled world we presently live in. Perhaps Master Jin's profound words will reach out and touch more of the uninitiated public, so that they are then drawn to and subsequently inspired to undertake a pursuit of the internal method in this unique and dynamic art.

In spirit with Sheng Jun and all the devotees of this tradition, I look forward to a wide dissemination of this publication and to the "unexpected results" for all our future practitioners. With sincerity and humility I add these few words.

Written the seventh month of 2014
Vincent Black of Tucson, Arizona
Sixty-three years of age

GENERAL CONCEPTS FOR COMPILING THIS VOLUME
[Preface to the 1930 edition]

THIS BOOK SPRINGS FROM the observations and guidance of Jin Yunting of Wuqiao. Although the compiler can awkwardly explain to practitioners each action and each movement of Xingyiquan's hand methods and stepping patterns, illustrated explanations of the subtleties can immediately lead to understanding; those without an instructor can become proficient as if following a master, while those who follow a master in practice can gain even more insight when reading it.

When studying boxing arts without a master as a guide, although one can practice following the photos, not all postures and movements can be correct. Therefore "postural corrections" and "rhyme songs" have been added after the illustrated explanations for each sequence in this book, to aid students in reaching some understanding through contemplation and recitation. Furthermore, photographs of Master Jin Yunting himself demonstrating important postures have been inserted among the illustrations to serve as a model.

This book is divided into two parts. The first part contains general theory relating to and recounting the origins of Xingyiquan, its content, and its application. The second part contains the boxing manual and the rhyme songs.

One name for this boxing style is Form Intention Five Element Boxing, and it is the initial level after entering the Wudang school. Its effects are similar to those of Springy Legs of the Shaolin school. Those things that develop from the transformations of the five elements include Five Element Connected Links, Twelve Shapes Two-Person Boxing, Five Element Creative/Destructive Boxing, and many others. These are all called Xingyi. The purpose of this book is to explore the fundamentals and to seek their origin, and so it compiles only the one category of the five elements;

additional publications for each of the other categories of boxing also should be undertaken .

In order for this boxing manual to allow the reader to clearly understand without faltering, each action and each movement has been laid out in illustrations but, in actuality, when practicing these must be unceasing and connected, before and after simultaneously, and cannot be ponderous and repeatedly halting as in the pictures. Students must feel this.

Although this book was compiled painstakingly, seeking the essence, and sent to press only after the corrections of several people, it is unavoidable to still have errors and omissions, and I pray that wise people throughout the country will provide comments and corrections for this work.

FOREWORD BY SHENG JUN

ASIDE FROM THE CULTIVATION of virtue and the cultivation of wisdom, I also value the cultivation of the body. There are many paths to cultivation of the body, but if you are seeking one that is simple and suitable for all ages, there is none like Xingyi boxing, because this art specifically takes *qi* cultivation as its foundation. Splitting, Smashing, Drilling, Pounding, and Crossing correspond to metal, wood, water, fire, and earth and divide externally into the five postures. Internally they fill the five organs and are the natural, profound way to health. Now Jin Yunting of Wuqiao is using these illustrations to demonstrate clearly, at great advantage to later generations, how easy it is! I began studying this art with Mr. Jin Yunting during the winter of the *xinyou* year [1921], and in less than twenty months I already feel that my body is strong and healthy through its [Xingyi's] exceptional protective benefits. I greatly look forward to the publishing and wide dissemination of this book, and cannot control my fervent wishes that numerous future students may research this physical cultivation and enter onto this right path.

Written the fifth month, *guihai* year [1923]
Sheng Jun (盛鈞), style name Weichen (蔚岑), of Wu County
Sixty-three years of age

Foreword by Zheng Guangzhao

A FTER THE REFORMS OF the *xinhai* year [the 1911 revolution], I moved to Shanghai to teach at the residence of Guardian[1] Sheng. There I met Mr. Jin Yunting of Wuqiao, who told me he had come from the north and was skilled in martial arts. I had no experience with this art, and my nature was not one to be drawn to these things, so I dismissed this and put it behind me. Now Mr. Wu Dicheng, style name Zhiting, and Mr. Lü Zibin both had stiff, weak bodies, but after studying for just more than one year, each felt that his body and qi were both truly changed. Because Dicheng and the others all realized Xingyi's efficacious nature, they recommended it to Mr. Cui Heqing. When his chronic asthma and exhausted body began to heal, he hastened his efforts and, in less than a year, all of his maladies had disappeared.

I found this quite remarkable and said to our teacher that he was not only good at fighting arts, but also skilled in healing arts. In answer, our teacher lectured us, saying:

> All of the martial arts in the world originated with Damo. Yue Wumu[2] of the Song Dynasty looked back to and combined the essence of the two classics written by Damo—the *Muscle-Tendon Changing Classic* and the *Marrow-Washing Classic*—to create Xingyi boxing. No matter whether you look at it straightforward or roundabout, complicated or confused, it all comes down to using the intention to create form, and using form to create qi. This is the essence of what I have learned.
>
> When I was young I engaged in business, and my body became weak and I had many illnesses. I was told that if I could obtain the teachings of Xingyi boxing, I could eradicate this weakness and illness, so I began searching for a teacher. Now, while those who are skilled in Shaolin or Wudang arts are numerous,

very few are skilled at Xingyi. Those who do know, if they are not arrogant, are tight-lipped, so I traveled around and around until I finally reached the two masters, Shang Yunxiang of Leling County and Sun Lutang of Wanping County, under whose guidance I traveled for more than ten years. I was able to glimpse their art, and although my own art is still not refined, my body is now without maladies.

I tell people that what I say to them is not deception. In fact, there is nothing outside the cultivation of qi. If you can nurture qi, your mind will be calm, you will be what people call "a gentleman of heavenly calm and composure," and your body will have no place for sickness. You say that I am skilled in the healing arts, but I dare not claim so.

I say that this is just my teacher's modesty and that, in fact, his words are a true understanding of the *Dao*, for though I have been associated with him for only several months, I feel that I am flourishing in my everyday life. Now our teacher has followed the requests of his compatriots to publish this volume. I present what I have heard and seen, briefly recounting it here as an addendum to the forewords of these other gentlemen. As for the illustrations and discussions, we have our teacher's original text, so I won't reiterate those here.

The eighth month, *guihai* year [1923]
Zheng Guangzhao (鄭光照), style name Yicang (逸蒼), of Wujin
Penned at the Yuzhai Study, Shanghai
Sixty-three years of age

Foreword by Sheng Yulin

Xingyi boxing is also called *Wuxing*[3] boxing and follows the principles of metal, wood, water, fire, and earth; heart, liver, spleen, lungs, kidneys [*sic*]; *yin* and *yang;* and movement and stillness. Not only is it an exceptional fighting art, but it also strengthens tendons and bones and enlivens the blood and vessels. Formerly I was plump and my movements hindered. Mr. Jin has trained me for two winters and summers without cease, and I now feel that my spirit is lively and my gait light and easy, proving that this boxing art has endless advantage for people in terms of physical cultivation. It should be regarded by all people as a great treasure. I submit these few words of record as accompaniment to the text.

Sheng Yulin (盛玉麐) of Wujin

FOREWORD BY CUI HEQING

X INGYI BOXING IS TRULY the essential art of physical cultivation. Practice requires perseverance, but if one practices daily without cease, power will fill the body and the results will exceed expectations. Before, I suffered from damp phlegm and shortness of breath, which medicine could not help. Many of my comrades recommended this art to me, and I took to the learning of Mr. Yunting, a man of sincere heart. After only one year, my body is now light and healthy, my vision and appetite superb. When drinking water, one should ponder its source. Truly this has been a gift from my teacher, so I write these few lines in appreciation of his superior conduct, and as a record, so that it will not be forgotten.

Written by Cui Heqing (崔鶴卿) of Wuqing, near the capital
Fifty-seven years of age

FOREWORD BY WU SHULAN

M Y BODY IS THIN but my spirit is fierce. In the winter of the *renzi* year [1912], I traveled north and suddenly developed a pulmonary hemorrhage. By the time this sickness healed, it had greatly injured my *yuan qi.*[4] With physical exertion I was winded, and medicine had no effect. This went on for several years, and although I was not old, I was already exhausted. This was very distressing.

Mr. Jin Yunting was a friend of mine from the same hometown, skilled in the art of Xingyi. In the seventh month of the *jiwei* year [1919], he came to Shanghai and expounded to me the mysteries of this art, which takes the creation of freely downward-flowing *qi* as its main principle. After fully filling the *dantian,* one can supplement deficiencies of both pre- and post-Heaven *qi.* If one studies this art, then one can receive the most benefits. Mr. Jin expounded most highly, and I suddenly saw the light. Following this, I met with Mr. Wu Dicheng and Mr. Lü Zibin and, in the ninth month of that year, I began studying.

Mr. Jin was skilled in giving systematic explanation and always taught without reserve. I trained continuously without cease, several times a day, and in less than five years, my old illness had been eradicated. Now I am fifty-two, and my body is healthier than before. My steps are as lively as those of a forty-year-old. As for Misters Wu and Lü, their health was originally better than mine and now is even stronger. With deep feeling I recount this and, with these few words, record it so that it will not be forgotten.

The fifth month, *guihai* year [1923]
Wu Shulan (吳樹蘭), style name Zhiting (芷庭), of Nangong, Hebei

FOREWORD BY WU DICHENG

XINGYI BOXING ORIGINATED WITH Damo, passed to Yue Wumu of the Song Dynasty, and during the great Ming period experienced continuous transmission, with branches spreading in abundance throughout the north. Even I had heard of it. Jin Yunting of Wuqiao is skilled in this art. In the autumn of the *jiwei* year [1919] he came to Shanghai, and once we met we became inseparable good friends. He then set forth his intention to make the dispelling of sickness and extension of life his goal. I myself had many sicknesses and therefore began studying. After only five winters and summers without cease I felt that, compared to before, my spirit and strength were like those of a completely different person. I then began to believe that Mr. Jin's words were not just exaggeration.

Subsequently I heard that he had a school brother who gave him the transmissions of their [martial arts] school, which had not yet been made public. I read this, which was on the whole concerned with cultivation of the body, the nurturing of *qi,* and how—if one is able to develop *qi*—the spirit will naturally become complete. I realized that this document is perfect for those who have interest but no way to proceed. Although its meaning is profound, the words are very clear; this art is suitable for young and old alike and helps one to attain benevolence and long life. I encouraged him [Jin Yunting] to publish this book for the benefit of others, and he agreed wholeheartedly. I have respectfully added this colophon of a few words to record something worthy of admiration.

The fifth month, *guihai* year [1923]
Written by Wu Dicheng (吳砥成) of Wu County, Jiangsu

FOREWORD BY LÜ ZIBIN

J IN YUNTING IS ORIGINALLY from Wuqiao, Hebei Province. As a young man, he studied under the famous teacher Shang Yunxiang and achieved great understanding after more than twenty years of researching Xingyi boxing. This art is divided into five fists: Splitting, which corresponds to metal; Smashing, which corresponds to wood; Drilling, which corresponds to water; Pounding, which corresponds to fire; and Crossing, which corresponds to earth. Its main aim is to nurture *qi* and develop the body, and is unconnected with fighting. It is said that the form circulates the intention; therefore it is called Xingyi. In the autumn of the *jiwei* year [1919], Fourth Master Zecheng began promoting physical education and invited Mr. Jin to Shanghai to teach his comrades. Mr. Jin was not vexed by repeated instruction and, in fact, was as comforting and friendly as a spring wind. I was formerly of weak constitution and always taking medicine, but after engaging in this practice for only a year, it was as if my sicknesses had disappeared. I now benefit from continued good health and deeply believe that the ancient worthies do not deceive us. I discussed with my teacher the possibility of reprinting this boxing treatise for compatriot fellows, and so that this national treasure of physical cultivation can be esteemed by people in the West. I now relate these origins as this printing nears completion.

The fifth month, *guihai* year [1923]
Lü Zibin (呂子彬), style name Wenwei (文蔚), of Ba County,
near the capital

FOREWORD BY QIAN YANTANG

IN THE PAST, MY father was a government official in the capital county. Now, it's known that northerners possess a very stubborn temperament, especially martial artists. When I was young I followed him to his post, and in my spare time, apart from hard studies, I enjoyed martial arts skill. Springy Legs, Shaolin, spear, lance, sword, and halberd—there was nothing in which I was not adept. Later I met Guo Yunshen of Shen County, Hebei Province, who said to me, "Rather than exert yourself with these lesser arts, why don't you devote your strength to a true teaching?" I then invited him to our residence with all the gifts appropriate for a teacher so that I might seek stillness in movement and achieve a superior level of fighting skill. After more than ten years of study, I suddenly realized that I had developed considerable qi and had received a considerable gift, and that his words were truly not empty. Now, though I have already passed middle age, my spirit is exceptional, and I feel contented. After returning south to live in Shanghai, I unexpectedly encountered Jin Yunting of Wuqiao, with whom I discussed this boxing art. I discovered that he was of the same lineage as myself, and after thoroughly questioning his origins, found that he was the prominent student of Shang Yunxiang of Leling County, Shandong Province. As a result of close association and deep, mutual admiration, various officials and a certain university in Shanghai invited Yunting to instruct students using Xingyi and other arts. Those who received these benefits joined their voices in lauding and praising him, and those calling at his door seeking instruction became more numerous by the day. He is currently a guest of Sheng Zecheng (盛澤承) of Wujin, who nearly a year ago invited him to teach at his residence, and where the number of those who come to study and benefit from this art has increased daily. Now, Yunting has illuminated the various postures of Xingyi using photoreproduction, amended basic explanations, and requested Mr. Ling Guiqing of Wuxing to organize and order this work for society's benefit, so that later practitioners may all receive the true teachings of this style, and all people may benefit and lengthen their life through contemplation and practice. As this book nears completion, I recount its origins with these simple words.

Eighteenth year of the republic [1929—from 1930 edition]
Autumn's Eve, *guihai* year [1923—from 1931 edition]
Qian Yantang (錢硯堂) of Hang County

FOREWORD BY LING GUIQING

THIS BOOK IS EDITED in tribute to Master Jin Yunting of Wuqiao, who is an inner-chamber disciple of famed masters Shang Yunxiang and Sun Lutang. He has studied and researched Xingyi, Taiji, and other arts for almost twenty years, and his achievements are truly deep. In the first years of the republic Sir Sheng of Wujin invited him to come to Shanghai to instruct his children. Master taught clearly and systematically, passing more than ten summers and winters as if they were one day. Of all of the Sheng family and its old friends who had long-standing or chronic diseases and who studied with him, if they could maintain belief and not slacken, practicing without cease, there were none who did not quickly flourish. Mr. Wu Dicheng, secretary to Sir Sheng, was one of them. In his youth he was frail of body with many illnesses, and thus timid and weak-willed. [After] studying Xingyiquan with Master for several years his body became healthy and his qi abundant and although this year he will be fifty he is like a person of twentysomething. The manager of our bureau Shen Junsheng (沈駿聲) had a long-standing stomach illness that, though not extremely intense, came and went, and that he considered especially troubling. Hearing of Master's reputation he respected him and, through Mr. Wu Dicheng's introduction, began to study Xingyiquan. After not even three months, his disease was cured and his conviction became even greater. He exhorted Master to write a book and print it to benefit the world. However, Master's teaching duties and various affairs were without pause. In the spring of this year Mr. Shen again invited Master to come to our office to instruct each day for one hour, and strongly persuaded me to join in. After one month I gained some understanding of the purpose of Xingyiquan, moving at will through hand positions and stepping postures. Master was pleased and addressed me saying, "You know all I have used to develop you so quickly; now I take the responsibility of editing this boxing into a book and hand it over to you."

I replied that I would solemnly take this command and withdrew to write this book, illustrating its principles and laying out its theory. After working painstakingly for another month, and only after seeking correction by taking a draft and presenting it before Master as well as Mr. Wu and Mr. Shen, did I begin to dare to send it to print and out into the world. The origin of this editing is thus; as for the origins and effects of Xingyiquan, these are related in detail in this writing, and I will not add redundancies here.

Ling Shanqing (凌善清)[5] of Wuxing
Written in the Editors Office of Great East Publishing
Twelfth month of the seventeenth year of the Republic [1928]

FOREWORD BY JIN YUNTING

MENGZI SAID: "Control your will and do not scatter your *qi*,"[6] because the mind and the qi show your inner state. The mind is the commander of the qi. The qi is the army of the mind. If I am a commander without troops, then when it comes time for battle, who would employ me? No matter what we attempt to do, even when the mind is set, if the *qi* is insufficient, then it must be that matters cannot succeed. Therefore, Mengzi also said: "I am good at nourishing my vast *qi*."[7] As a youth, my constitution was weak, I was often sick, and could not endure physical labor. Some people enjoined me to use Xingyi boxing—which has the main aim of nurturing qi—as a restorative method, for if the qi is sufficient, the body is healthy and sickness will depart. Accordingly, I sought those skilled in this art and found Master Shang Yunxiang of Leling, and Master Sun Lutang of Wanping, under whose guidance I studied for more than ten years. Not only was my sickness healed, but my constitution became very strong through the exceptional protective benefits of this art.

Xingyi boxing originated with the founding master Damo, and from Henan came to Beijing. It is simple and uncomplicated, refined and not crude, easily understood, strenuous but not harmful. If practiced daily according to the proper theories, it will quickly cause tight sinews to stretch, the slack to draw in, the separated to unite, and the soft to become firm, and it will enliven the blood and vessels and strengthen the spirit. Needless to say, it may be practiced by both young and old without difficulty. During the autumn of the *jiwei* year [1919], Fourth Master Sheng Zecheng invited me to Shanghai. Those comrades who undertook to research this health-building and nourishing art did not abandon it, gathering together morning and night, and have now studied ten years. In the spring of this year, Mr. Wu Dicheng and Mr. Shen Junsheng repeatedly urged and enjoined me to pass on this method as sustenance for those to come. Because I received a positive response from Great East Publishing's Editorial Director Mr. Ling Guiqing, I asked him to create drawings and lay down these principles in print to popularize them to the world. To avoid seeming ignorant, I attach these few sentences to seek guidance from contemporary gentlemen of true skill.

Written by Jin Yunting (靳雲亭), style name Zhenqi (振起), of Wuqiao

SUMMARY OF THE FIVE PRINCIPLES

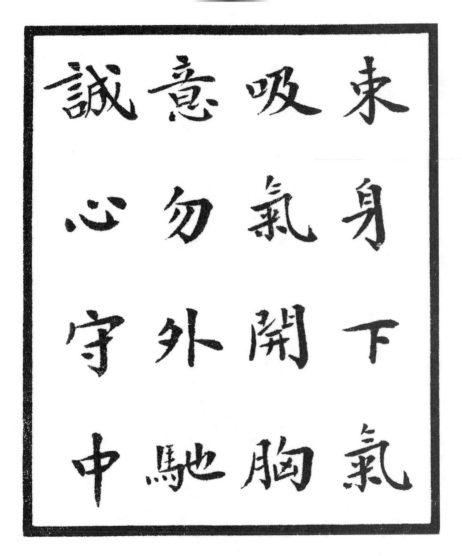

誠意吸束
心勿氣身
守外開下
中馳胸氣

Calm the body and sink the *qi*.
Inhale and open the chest.
The intention does not wander.
With sincerity of heart, maintain the center.

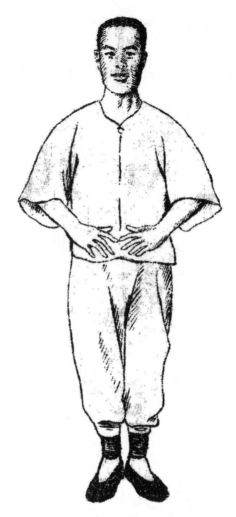

Preparatory Posture

Beneficial in nourishing vast *qi*.
Continually intone the Wisdom Sutra.[8]
Above, middle, and below, the *qi* settles.
The body, hands, and feet are aligned and true.

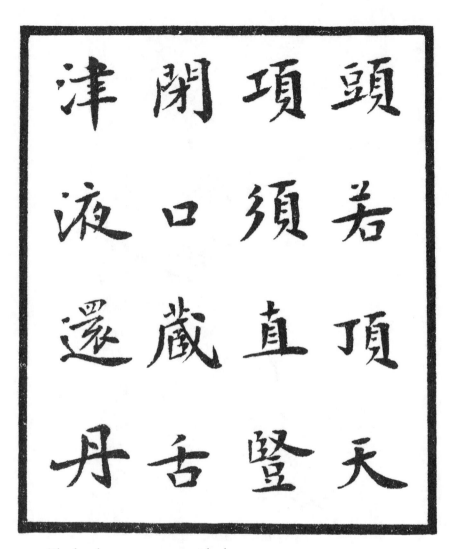

頭若頂天

項須直豎

閉口藏舌

津液還丹

The head seems to press to the heavens.
The nape of the neck must be straight and erect.
Close the mouth and hide the tongue.
So the *jin* and *ye*[9] can return to the *dantian*.

Pi Quan—Splitting Fist

The first is called Splitting.

Its form is like an axe.

It corresponds to the metal element.

Of the *zang* organs, it nourishes the lungs.

Using the fist, it must clench tightly.

Using the palm, it must have *qi*.

Do not bend forward or lean back.

Do not tilt to the left or slant to the right.

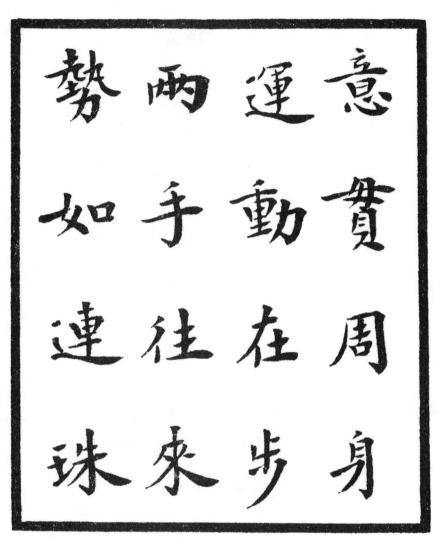

The intention fills the entire body.
Movement is in the footwork.
The two hands come and go.
The postures are like a string of pearls.

Beng Quan—Smashing Fist

The second[10] is called Smashing.

Its form is like an arrow.

It corresponds to the wood element.

Of the *zang* organs, it calms the liver.

The front foot should not hook in and must not turn out.

The back foot seems straight, but is not straight; seems turned
   out, but is not turned out.

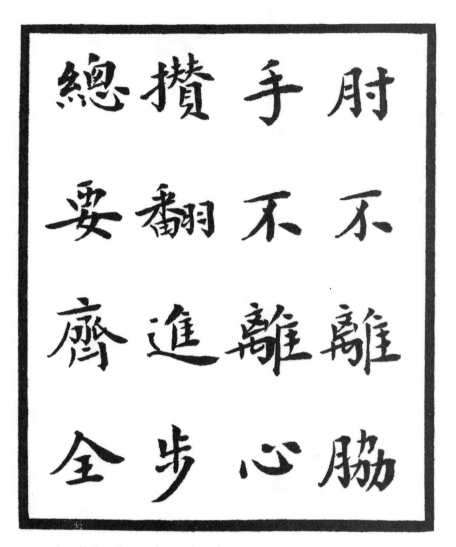

總攬要齊全
攬翻進步
手不離心
肘不離脅

The elbows do not leave the ribs.
The hands do not leave the heart.
Drill, overturn, and advance.
Always uniting the whole.

Zuan Quan—Drilling Fist

The third is called Drilling.

Its form is like lightning.

It corresponds to the water element.

Of the *zang* organs, it supplements the kidneys.

The two legs and two arms seem straight but are not straight;
seem bent, but are not bent.

There is *yin* and there is *yang*, but the central *qi* is stable.

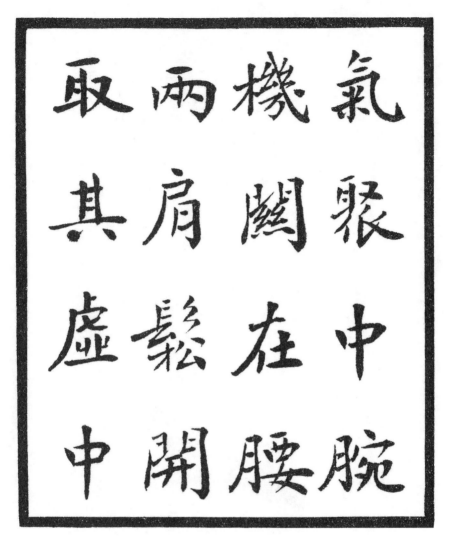

The *qi* gathers at *zhongwan*.[11]
The mechanism is in the waist.
The two shoulders relax and open
To seek its hollowness.

Pao Quan—Pounding Fist

The fourth is called Pounding.

Its form is like a cannon.

It corresponds to the fire element.

Of the *zang* organs, it nourishes the heart.

If hard then empty and insubstantial; if soft then heavy and solid.

Heavy and solid like a mountain, the *qi* penetrates the flesh.

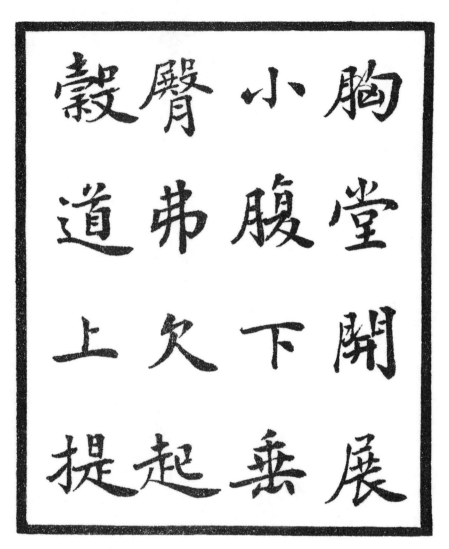

The chest cavity expands.
The abdomen sinks.
The buttocks do not rise up
And the anus is lifted.

Heng Quan—Crossing Fist

The fifth is called Crossing.

Its form is like a spring.

It corresponds to the earth element.

Of the *zang* organs, it nourishes the spleen.

Twist the body with the footwork; the shape is like twisted yarn.

The inside opening and the outside closing is called closing the
   chest.

Xingyiquan Lineage Chart

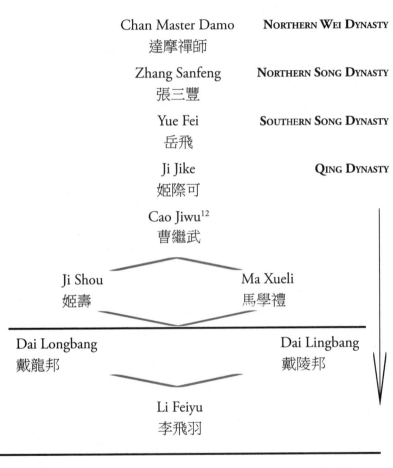

Chan Master Damo
達摩禪師
NORTHERN WEI DYNASTY

Zhang Sanfeng
張三豐
NORTHERN SONG DYNASTY

Yue Fei
岳飛
SOUTHERN SONG DYNASTY

Ji Jike
姬際可
QING DYNASTY

Cao Jiwu[12]
曹繼武

Ji Shou　　　　　　　　　　Ma Xueli
姬壽　　　　　　　　　　　馬學禮

Dai Longbang　　　　　　　　　　Dai Lingbang
戴龍邦　　　　　　　　　　　　戴陵邦

Li Feiyu
李飛羽

Bai Xiyuan　Guo Yunshen　Liu Qilan　Che Yonghong　Song Shirong
白西園　　　郭雲深　　　劉奇蘭　　　車永鴻　　　　宋世榮

Xingyiquan Lineage Chart

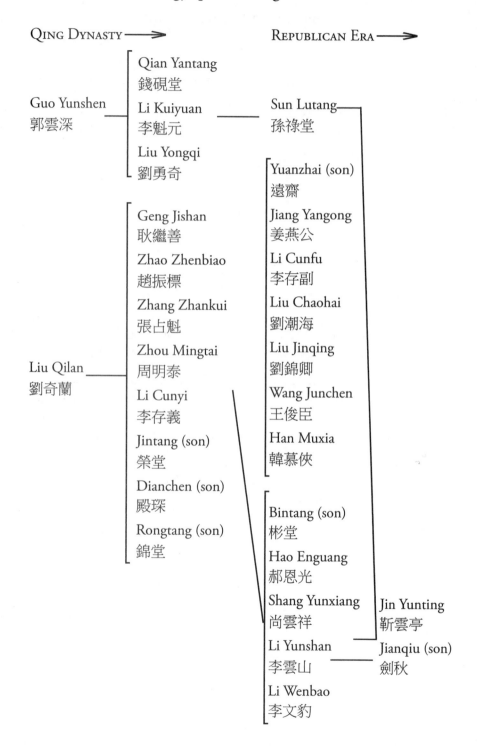

Guo Yunshen
郭雲深

  Qian Yantang
  錢硯堂

  Li Kuiyuan
  李魁元

  Liu Yongqi
  劉勇奇

Sun Lutang
孫祿堂

  Yuanzhai (son)
  遠齋

Liu Qilan
劉奇蘭

  Geng Jishan
  耿繼善

  Zhao Zhenbiao
  趙振標

  Zhang Zhankui
  張占魁

  Zhou Mingtai
  周明泰

  Li Cunyi
  李存義

  Jintang (son)
  榮堂

  Dianchen (son)
  殿琛

  Rongtang (son)
  錦堂

Jiang Yangong
姜燕公

Li Cunfu
李存副

Liu Chaohai
劉潮海

Liu Jinqing
劉錦卿

Wang Junchen
王俊臣

Han Muxia
韓慕俠

Bintang (son)
彬堂

Hao Enguang
郝恩光

Shang Yunxiang
尚雲祥

Li Yunshan
李雲山

Li Wenbao
李文豹

Jin Yunting
靳雲亭

Jianqiu (son)
劍秋

General Theory

The Origins of Xingyiquan

THE ARTS OF PUGILISM and wrestling have been esteemed by my country since antiquity. The *Guanzi* says: "Is there anyone in your dependencies who is energetic, courageous, and strong of limb, and whose muscles and bones make him stand out in a crowd? If there is, hereby report it,"[13] and the *Xunzi* states: "The men of Qi stress skill in hand-to-hand combat."[14] The *Book of Han* also says: "[King] Min of Qi employed pugilism to strengthen."[15] These are all proof of this.

At the time of the Six Dynasties, the Indian monk Damo carried with him his so-called "western regions" pugilism and began transmitting it in the central lands. Thereupon, athletic northerners rallied together and pursued it. Today, arts called Damo Boxing, Damo Sword, and others are still passed on in the world. Xingyiquan is one of these. From antiquity, all of the martial arts skills transmitted in my country mostly tend toward application, but what was transmitted by Damo focuses intention on cultivating life, and application is secondary. The name "Xingyiquan" is transliterated from Sanskrit. Its main purpose is focused on cultivating qi; therefore, at the time it was rather highly valued, and having been passed on to the present time has still been able to retain this original meaning. During the *Putong* reign period [520–527] of the Liang Dynasty, Damo crossed the river and traveled to Wei, establishing himself at Songshan Shaolin Temple, facing the wall for nine years before passing away. The temple monks obtained his complete corpus, blending and synthesizing it again with existing Chinese martial arts skills, transcending and reaching new heights, using it to surpass others; thereupon, what is called Shaolin boxing became well known throughout the world, spreading further day by day the meaning of all that was taught by Damo.

In the era of the Northern Song, Zhang Sanfeng secluded himself in Wudang as a Daoist and wholeheartedly researched the arts of Damo for several years. After obtaining their profundity, he then completely set aside the conventions of Shaolin and took training qi as his single focus. Those who followed him received Xingyiquan as foundational-level training, and its effects were evident. Students swarmed forth, and commoners eventually named this the "internal school" and called Shaolin the "external school," with Xingyi at this time gradually becoming something particular to the internal family. In the Song Dynasty, this crossed into the south, where Yue Fei—assembling compatriots from far-flung hamlets to train fist and poles as a defense against the Jin—aspired to obtain and perfect the Xingyiquan of the "Wudang school," authoring a manual that elucidated its broad principles; thereby, the achievements of Xingyiquan became even more significant.

After this, [Xingyiquan was passed on] from the Song to the Yuan, and from the Yuan to the Ming. Although every generation had its inheritors, their names are not clear, and there are no trails to investigate. Arriving at the beginning of the Qing Dynasty, there was Ji Jike, style name Longfeng, of Zhufeng, Pudong, who visited famous masters between Sichuan and Shanxi, and obtained the Wumu boxing manual in Zhongnan, researching it and perfecting the art, and later teaching his disciple Cao Jiwu. Jiwu taught Ji Shou, who wrote a preface to the Wumu manual and published it for the world. At the same time, in Luoyang, Ma Xueli studied secretly with Jiwu, also obtaining this teaching, and becoming famous north and south of the great river.

During the *Xianfeng* reign period, Dai Longbang and his younger brother [Dai] Lingbang of Qi County both received instruction from Xueli;[16] both their achievements were profound, their names shaking all of Shanxi Province. At the end of the Tongzhi reign period, Li Neng[17] of Shenzhou heard of the reputations of the [Dai brothers] and traveled especially to Shanxi to visit them. Admiring their art, [Li Neng] studied it for nine years until his skill was complete; then he returned east, establishing a school and accepting disciples. Those from afar who followed him were numerous, and it was from this time that Hebei began to have Xingyiquan.

When Li [Neng] died, his disciples Liu Qilan, Guo Yunshen, Che Yonghong, Song Shirong, and Bai Xiyuan were all able to carry on his teachings. Liu Qilan passed this on to his sons, Jintang, Dianchen, and Rongtang, as well as to his disciples Li Cunyi, Zhou Mingtai, Zhang Zhankui, Zhao Zhenbiao, and Geng Jishan.

Guo Yunshen transmitted it to Liu Yongqi and Li Kuiyuan.

Li Cunyi passed it on to Shang Yunxiang, Li Wenbao, Li Yunshan, Hao Enguang, and his son Bintang.

Zhang Zhankui passed it on to Han Muxia and Wang Junchen, Liu Jinqing, Liu Chaohai, Li Cunfu, and his son Yuanqi.

Li Kuiyuan passed it on to Sun Lutang.

Li Yunshan transmitted it to his son Jianqiu.

Shang Yunxiang passed it on to Jin Yunting of Wuqiao, the driving force behind the editing of this book.

In the first year of the republic, one after the other, Jin Yunting and Li Jianqiu traveled south, writing about, expressing ideas on, and promoting this art, following the gathering energy in vogue at the time north and south of the great river. In the seventeenth year of the republic, the National Revolutionary Army succeeded in striking north, establishing a capital in Nanjing, and ordering an academy to be built to encourage the national arts. Because of its [origins in the] distant past and its long transmission, its simple methods, and its profound meaning, no effort was spared in promoting [Xingyi] boxing. Following this, should this boxing not be spread so that all households know of it as the foundation for a strong nation and strong people? My heart prays for this! On tiptoes I look for it!

An Explanation of Xingyi

Xing is form and image. Yi is the mind's intention. Humans are the most intelligent of the ten thousand things, and can feel and understand the reactions of all things. Thus, although the mind is internal, the principles are in all things, and although the things are external, the principles are contained in the mind. Intention is the expression of the mind. Therefore, if the mind and intention are sincere internally, and the ten thousand things are formed externally, internal and external are felt together, and do not depart from the flowing of a unified qi. Therefore, in originating and creating this boxing, founding master Damo's tenet was in cultivating qi in order to benefit strength, using simple movements but [gaining] inexhaustible benefits, and he thus called it Form Intention Boxing.

Xingyiquan's One *Qi*

The Taiji originally is undifferentiated, without shape and without intention, but within it is contained one unified qi. This qi circulates within the universe, there is nowhere it does not reach, and it is the core of all living things. What is called "one qi" is also called congenital true unified qi. From this qi are born the two principles; Heaven and earth begin to be differentiated, Yin and yang begin to be distinguished, and humanity is also produced as a result of this. Therefore, this qi actually is the root of life, the fountainhead of creation, and the basis for life and death. If one is able to cultivate this qi and maintain it without losing it, then one will be long-lived. If one cuts it off and loses it, following its scattering is an untimely death. Xingyiquan utilizes exercises developed by people to combine yin and yang and to unite nature, desiring to turn yang to yin, and to return from acquired to congenital, maintaining this qi and causing it to advance into the golden years. Therefore, if one speaks of it in summary, the ten thousand changes of position and the hundred layers of mystery within this boxing do not stray from the two words "training breath."

Xingyiquan's Two Principles

The two principles are born of the unified qi—they are Heaven and earth. They are also yin and yang. If there is only yang, then there is no creation. If only yin, then there is no continuation. Yin and yang blend, and the ten thousand things are created. This is the natural principle of Heaven and earth. Human life is also a small Heaven and earth. Everywhere within the four limbs and within each and every movement, there is not one thing that cannot be divided into yin and yang. If yin and yang are harmonized, then the body is healthy and movements are flowing. If yin and yang are unbalanced, then the body is weak and movements will become abnormal. Now yin and yang are born from congenital true unified qi. If one wishes to cultivate this congenital true unified qi and to maintain it without losing it, one must first begin with regulating yin and yang. Those who study Xingyiquan cannot be unaware of the two principles. If we speak of the body, then the shoulders are yang, and the hips are yin. The shoulders must harmonize with the hips; this is the harmonizing of yin and yang. (The shoulders harmonizing wit the hips, the elbows harmonizing with the knees, and the hands harmonizing with the feet are the three external harmonies. See Xingyiquan's Six Harmonies later in this book.) The elbows are yang, and the knees are yin. The elbows and knees must be harmonized so that yin and yang are harmonized. The hands are yang and the feet are yin. If the hands and feet are harmonized, then yin and yang are balanced. When talking about movement, extension is yang and contraction is yin. Rising is yang and falling is yin. Extending and contracting naturally, rising and falling appropriately, are also ways to say yin and yang harmonizing. Within yin there is yang, and within yang there is yin. When yin reaches its extreme it produces yang, and when yang reaches its extreme it produces yin, crisscrossing and changing but unable to reach an end. Students must feel this within their bodies and clearly deliberate on it.

Xingyiquan's Three Bodies

The three bodies are the image of the three powers: Heaven, earth, and human. In boxing these are the head, hands, and feet. The three bodies are each divided into three segments, and are united internally and externally. The head is the root segment; outside is the head, inside is *niwan*.[18] The back is the middle segment; outside is the back, inside is the heart. The waist is the tip segment; outside is the waist, inside is the dantian. Similarly, the shoulders are the root segment, the elbows are the middle segment, and the hands are the tip segment; and the hips are the root segment, the knees are the middle segment, and the feet are the tip segment. Each of these three segments also has three segments. This theory corresponds with the numerology of nine found within the six [Confucian] classics. The *Book of Alchemy* speaks exactly of this when it says: "Out of emptiness and nothingness the Dao produces the one qi, and from the one qi arise yin and yang. Yin and yang again unite to form the three bodies, and when the three bodies are reborn the ten thousand things flourish."

Xingyiquan's Four Methods

Of the four methods of Xingyiquan, the first is called body methods; the second is called hand methods; the third is called foot methods; and the fourth is called stepping methods.

Body methods: One cannot tilt forward or lean back, [nor] slant left or incline right. Advance forward straight ahead, and retreat to the rear in a straight line.

Hand methods: The energy is in the wrists, the power is in the fingers. Turn and move with liveliness; open and close at will.

Foot methods: The foot drills as it rises and overturns as it falls. When not drilling or falling, first move one *cun*.[19]

Stepping methods include the three methods of inch stepping, fast stepping, and drilling stepping. Inch stepping is expanding the body and using inch power to advance quickly, the back foot pressing, the front foot advancing first, without changing stances. Fast stepping is horse-stance stepping, and relies completely on using power from the rear foot. This is what is described as "all information relies on rear foot pressing." Drilling stepping is when one foot advances straight forward and the rear foot follows. Compared to the two other styles of inch stepping and fast stepping, drilling stepping is the most common, and of the three methods is the most crucial.

Xingyiquan's Five Principles

Splitting Fist corresponds to metal and cultivates the lungs. If its energy is flowing, the lung qi will be harmonized. All people rely on qi as their foundation; if the qi is harmonized, then the body will naturally be strong.

Drilling Fist corresponds to water and supplements the kidneys. The movement of its qi is like the winding flowing of water; there is nowhere it does not reach. If its qi is harmonized, then the kidneys will be full, the clear qi will ascend, and the turbid qi will descend.

Smashing Fist corresponds to wood and calms the liver. It is the extension and contraction of a unified qi. If this fist is fluid, then the liver is calm, and one can increase the spirit, strengthen the tendons and bones, and solidify mental abilities.

Pounding Fist corresponds to fire and cultivates the heart. It is the opening and closing of a unified qi like the rending of a cannon blast. If its qi is harmonized, then the heart will be empty and numinous and the body relaxed and calm.

Crossing Fist corresponds to earth, and cultivate the spleen and harmonizes the stomach, and is the gathering of a unified qi. If its form is round, its nature is full, and its qi is flowing, then the five elements are harmonious and the hundred things can develop.

The form of Splitting Fist is like an axe, and thus corresponds to metal. The form of Drilling Fist is like electricity, and so corresponds to water. The form of Smashing Fist is like an arrow, and so corresponds to wood. The form of Pounding Fist is like a cannon, and so corresponds to fire. The form of Crossing Fist is like a spring, and so corresponds to earth. According to the theory of mutual creation, Splitting Fist gives rise to Drilling Fist, Drilling Fist gives rise to Smashing Fist, Smashing Fist gives rise to Pounding Fist, Pounding Fist gives rise to Crossing Fist, and Crossing Fist gives rise to Splitting Fist. According to the theory of mutual overcoming, Splitting Fist can overcome Smashing Fist, Smashing Fist can overcome Crossing Fist, Crossing Fist can overcome Drilling Fist, Drilling Fist can overcome Pounding Fist, and Pounding Fist can overcome Splitting Fist.

Xingyiquan's Six Harmonies

The most important point in Xingyiquan is in the word "harmonizing." If the movements are harmonized, then the postures are correct and preserve their benefit. If the movements are not harmonized, the postures are incorrect and the qi and power are useless. This cannot be disregarded. There are six so-called harmonies. The body not leaning (also expressed as "cannot be inclined"), the mind calm, the qi balanced, the intention not wandering, and the movements natural is called "the mind harmonized with the intent, the intent harmonized with the qi, the qi harmonized with the power." These are the internal three harmonies. When moving, the energy of the two hands hooking and the energy of the heels of the two feet twisting outward is called "the hands harmonized with the feet." The energy of the two elbows dropping downward and the energy of the two knees wrapping and hooking is called "the elbows harmonized with the knees." The two shoulders relaxed and open with pulling energy and the two hips wrapping at the root with pulling energy is called "the shoulders harmonized with the hips." These are the external three harmonies. Together they are called the six harmonies. If students can know the methods of the six harmonies well, then when practicing they may know one but infer many, and with each and every movement there will be none that are not consistent with the methods. Now aside from the [primary] internal three harmonies, still it must be that the mind harmonizes with the eyes, the liver harmonizes with the tendons, the spleen harmonizes with the muscles, the lungs harmonize with the body, and the kidneys harmonize with the bones. Aside from the [primary] external three harmonies, further it must be that the head harmonizes with the hands, the hands harmonize with the body, and the body harmonizes with the stepping. Observing this, one can know that within the movements of Xingyiquan, whether internal or external, there is nothing that does not possess the differentiation of yin and yang, and nothing that does not contain the principle of being mutually united. Students should attain this through their own bodily experience.

Xingyiquan's Seven Quicknesses

The seven quicknesses are: the eyes must be quick, the hands must be quick, the feet must be quick, the intention must be quick, issuing force must be quick, advancing and retreating must be quick, and the body method must be quick. Only when those who study boxing embody all of these seven quicknesses can they completely subdue others and be victorious. That which is described as crisscrossing and coming and going so that the eyes cannot follow, flashing like a dragon or tiger and causing others to be unable to follow, depends solely on these [seven quicknesses].

First, the eyes must be quick. The eyes are the sprouts of the mind. The eyes scrutinize the enemy's state and understand it in the mind, and then one is able to respond to the changes of the enemy and succeed in snatching victory. The [boxing] manual says: "The mind is the commander, the eyes are the vanguard." This describes that the mind is the leader and that it relies solely upon the slowness or quickness of eye movement.

Second, the hands must be quick. The hands are a human's wings. Whether guarding and covering, or advancing to attack, there is nothing that does not depend on them. However, the way of crossing hands depends on slowness or quickness. Slowness is losing, quickness is winning; this principle is natural. Therefore, a common saying is: "The eyes bright and the hands quick, attaining victory without defeat." And the [boxing] manual says: "The hands rise like arrows and fall like the wind, chasing the wind and pursuing the moon without relenting." This is also called "hand methods nimble and quick." Taking advantage of [the enemy's] unpreparedness and attacking, coming out of their inattentiveness and reaching them, not fearing the enemy's large size or ferocious power, one can issue hands like the wind and can be victorious over others.

Third, the feet must be quick. The feet are the foundation of the body. If the feet are set stably, then the body is stable. If the feet advance forward, then the body follows them. In Xingyiquan the entire body conveys power equally, and there is no place that is overweighted. The feet advance and the body advances, stealing the position of the opponent, who will naturally be knocked down. The [boxing] manual says: "The feet strike and tread, the intention does not show the emotions; information relies solely on the rear foot pressing; the foot treads the central gate, stealing the position; these magical hands are difficult to defend against." It also says: "The feet strike seventy percent, the hands strike thirty." From this point of view, the quickness of the feet must be even faster than the quickness of the hands.

Fourth, the intention must be quick. The intention is the commander of the body. The eyes have the skill of controlling, the hands have the ability to engage, and the feet have the skill to move, yet their slowness or quickness, tightness or laxity, all follow the intention. This is what is called establishing the intention with one quickness, so that the eyes, hands, and feet all achieve their essential requirements. Therefore, the clarity of the eyes inspecting the smallest detail is caused by the intention. The hands issuing and not coming back empty is caused by the intention. The agility of the feet is also caused by the intention. Seeing this, one can know that intention must be quick.

Fifth, issuing force must be quick. What is stored within is intention. What is manifested externally is the force. If the intention is quick, then even more so issuing force must be quick. In the moment as events arise, it must be that the force arises following the intention. Following the opportunity and changing accordingly, like a sudden thunder strike, the opponent cannot cover their ears in time, causing them to be flustered and confused with no way to withstand it; only then can one create victory. If the intention changes very rapidly and the force is not quick enough to follow it, then responding will be abnormal and one's defeat must be certain. Therefore, if intention and force are united, success can be certain; if the intention is quick but the force is slow, then defeat is without doubt. Those who study fighting surely must pay close attention to this.

Sixth, advancing and retreating must be quick. The theories in this section are the methods of crisscrossing, coming and going, advancing and retreating, turning and flanking. When it is time to advance, then advance, exhausting [the opponent's] power and advancing straight. When it is time to retreat, then retreat, guiding their qi and then returning it to them. Regarding the suitability of advancing or retreating, one must observe the strengths and weaknesses of the enemy. If strong, then avoid them and use cleverness to reach them. If weak, then attack them and use power to check them. Quickly advancing and quickly retreating, not allowing the opponent to take advantage of their opportunities, is what is called "following the timing high and low, crisscrossing according to the force."

Seventh, the body method must be quick. Within the martial art of Xingyiquan, all methods such as the five elements, six harmonies, seven quicknesses, and eight requirements utilize body method at their core. The [boxing] manual says: "The body is like the bow and the fists are like the arrows." It also says: "The advancing method requires first advancing the body, and when hands and feet arrive together only then is it true." Therefore, body method is the core of the art of Xingyiquan. Waving the shoulders and enlivening the hips, the entire body turns, flanking with the body and advancing, not bending forward or leaning back, slanting left or tilting right. When advancing, issue straight out; when retreating, set down straight. One must especially pay close attention until the internal and external are harmonized, causing the entire body above and below to unite as one. Although advancing and retreating cannot be loose and disorganized, they should not be expected, so that the enemy cannot succeed in their ill intent. In addition to the eyes being quick and the hands being quick, it is especially important for the body to be quick.

Xingyiquan's Seven Flowings

The shoulders must propel the elbows, but the elbows must not counteract the shoulders. The elbows must propel the hands, but the hands must not counteract the elbows. The hands must propel the fingers but the fingers must not counteract the hands. The waist must propel the hips, but the hips must not counteract the waist. The hips must propel the knees, but the knees must not counteract the hips. The knees must propel the feet, but the feet must not counteract the knees. The head must propel the body, but the body must not counteract the head. The heart qi even and calm, yin and yang united (for all parts of the limbs and the body, extending is yang and contracting is yin), above and below connected, internal and external as one: these are called the seven flowings.

Xingyiquan's Eight Postures

There are eight important points regarding the postures of Xingyiquan. First is pressing, second is lifting, third is hooking, fourth is rounding, fifth is holding, and sixth is falling. The seventh, crossing and following, must be clearly known. The eighth, rising, drilling, falling, and overturning, must be clearly separated. Pressing means the head pressing upward, the tip of the tongue pressing against the hard palate, and the hands pressing outward. Lifting means the coccyx lifting upward (thus pressing the back outward), and the anus lifting inward (causing *yang qi* to rise up the Du meridian). Hooking means the chest must hook (opening the chest to smooth the qi, allowing *yin qi* to descend the Ren meridian), the backs of the hands must hook, and the soles of the feet must hook downward. Rounding means the spine must round, the tiger's mouth must be half round, the arms must have a crescent shape, the wrists must press outward with a crescent shape, and the legs are connected and bent and must have a crescent shape. Holding means the dantian must hold, the mind must hold, and the arms must hold. Falling means the qi falls to the dantian, the tips of the shoulders fall downward, and the points of the elbows fall downward. Crossing is rising; following is falling. Rising is drilling; falling is overturning. Rising is the beginning of crossing; drilling is the completion of crossing. Falling is the beginning of following; overturning is the completion of following. The hands rise and drill and fall and overturn. The feet rise and drill and fall and overturn. Rising is issuing out; falling is striking. Rising is also striking; falling is also striking. Regardless of how one rises and falls, drills and overturns, or comes and goes, it always must be that the elbows do not leave the ribs, and the hands do not leave the heart. These are all of the postural elements of Xingyiquan that should be paid attention to.

Xingyiquan's Eight Requirements

What are the eight requirements? First, the internal must lift. Second, the three centers must join. Third, the three intentions must connect. Fourth, the five elements must flow. Fifth, the four termini must arrive together. Sixth, the mind must be at ease. Seventh, the three tips must align. Eighth, the eyes must be poisonous.

The internal must lift: Tightly gather the anus and lift the qi, causing it to ascend and to gather in the dantian, and then cause the qi gathered in the dantian to pass straight up the spine until the qi reaches the top of the head, circulating cyclically everywhere without cease. This is what is referred to by: "Tightly close the anus and lift internally."

The three centers must join: The top center of the head moves downward, the centers of the feet move upward, and the centers of the hands move backward. The reason for these three is to cause qi to gather in one place. If the top center of the head does not move downward, then the ascending qi cannot enter the dantian. If the centers of the feet do not move upward, then the descending qi cannot be collected in the dantian. If the centers of the hands do not move backward, then the external qi cannot be condensed in the dantian. Therefore, the three centers must join so that qi can begin to gather as one.

The three intentions must connect: The mind intention, the qi intention, and the power intention connect as one. These are called the internal three harmonies. These three utilize the mind as the strategist, the qi as the commander, and the power as the officers and infantry. If the qi is not full, then the power is insufficient; although the mind may have a plan, it is useless. Therefore, if qi intention is trained well, later one may externally command the power intention and internally accord with the mind intention. In connecting the three intentions, one should especially regard qi as the first concern.

The five elements must flow: The external five elements are the five fists: Splitting, Smashing, Pounding, Drilling, and Crossing. The internal five elements are the five zang organs: heart, liver, spleen, lungs, and kidneys.[20] The five fists of the external five elements change in application, each flowing in its sequence, so that amid chaos and uncertainty will be order and exactness. Anywhere the qi and power arrive, the postures follow them. Anywhere the postures reach, the qi and power guide them. If qi and power are ample, then the postures will be efficacious, and training the postures will increase qi and power. Therefore, the five elements must flow in order for the qi to flow.

The four termini must arrive together: The tongue [tip] must push up, the teeth must be clenched, the fingers and toes must hook, and the pores must close. When the tongue [tip] presses against the [palate], *jinye* fluids fill upward, and the qi and the blood circulate freely. When the teeth are clenched, the qi fills the bones and marrow. When the fingers and toes hook inward, the qi infuses the tendons. When the pores are closed, the qi of the entire body gathers and solidifies. To implement the arriving together, every time one takes a posture, the tongue presses, the teeth clench, the fingers and toes hook, and the pores close all as one mechanism, without differentiation between first and last, slow and fast. When employing the four termini, if there is any deficiency then the qi will scatter and the power will be slack, and thus be insufficient [for] fighting.

The mind must be at ease: During training the mind cannot be flustered or hurried. When flustered, one has a frightened and fearful intention. When hurried, one has an anxious and hasty intention. When [one is] frightened and fearful, the qi will be dispirited. When [one is] anxious and hasty, the qi will be chaotic. When [the qi is] dispirited and chaotic, there is nothing that the hands and feet can accomplish. If [the qi is] like on a normal day when not practicing, then internally one will be deficient and empty; in meeting situations one will be timid and shrinking. When approaching an enemy, one must not be fearful and frightened, [or] anxious and hasty. Therefore, the mind must be at ease and be full with trained qi externally and internally.

The three tips must align: The tip of the nose, the tip of the hand, and the tip of the foot must align. If the hand does not align with the nose but is shifted to the left, then the right-side blocking methods will be empty. If shifted to the right, then left-side blocking methods will be empty. If the hand and the foot, [or] the foot and the nose, are not aligned, the danger is the same. Moreover, if all three are shifted and are misaligned excessively, then the entire body cannot use power evenly, and certainly cannot join together as one; because of this, the qi will be scattered: Although the top center of the head moves downward, the qi will not change to moving downward. Although the centers of the feet move upward, the qi will not change to collecting upward. Although the [centers of the] hands move backward, the qi will not change to contracting inward. This is a natural principle. Therefore, when the three tips are not aligned, it will truly be a great hindrance and an obstruction to training qi.

The eyes must be poisonous: The light of the eyes is penetrating and threatening. The word "poisonous" means threatening, serious, quick, and agile. Those without ample original qi cannot attain this. Studying boxing arts does not stray from training the qi and training power. Training power can build the body; training the qi can extend the spirit. Those with profound *gongfu* are able to condense the dantian and to relax and open the zang organs. Their spirit must be lively, their cognitive power must be ample and full, their ears, eyes, mouth, nose, and other organs must be able to be fully utilized, and their eyes especially must be spirited and grand with rays of light penetrating others. This is what is called poisonous.

Xingyiquan's Nine Songs

Body: Bending forward or leaning back, the stance is not energized. Tilting left or slanting right are both illnesses of the body. Be upright but seemingly inclined, inclined but seemingly upright.

Shoulders: The head should press upward; the shoulders should sink downward. The left shoulder forms a bend, and the right shoulder follows naturally. Bringing the body's power to the hands is the function of the shoulders.

Arms: The left arm extends forward, the right arm is at the ribs, seemingly bent but not bent, seemingly straight but not straight. If too bent, then not far enough; if too straight, then diminished power.

Hands: The right hand is at the ribs, the left hand is at the level of the chest, the rear slightly sinking, the front extending power forward. The two hands are overturned; the use of power should be even.

Fingers: The five fingers are separated, their forms like hooks. The tiger's mouth is rounded and full, seemingly hard and seemingly soft. The power should reach the fingers, but cannot be sought forcefully.

Thighs: The left thigh is in front, the right thigh is in back, pressing as if straight but not straight, as if bent but not bent. Although containing straight and bent, always exhibiting chicken form.

Feet: The left foot is straight forward; angled and turned are both sicknesses. The right foot posture is angled. The front heel is aligned to the shin, the distance according to the person, the toes hooking firmly.

Tongue: The tongue is the terminus of the muscles. If [the tongue is] curled up, the qi descends. The eyes are wide, the hair is on end, the dantian feels heavier, the muscles are like steel, internally strengthening the *zang-fu* organs.

Buttocks: Lift the buttocks, and the qi will penetrate the four termini. When the two legs spiral, the muscles of the buttocks join. If [the buttocks are] low, the postures will be scattered; therefore, [the buttocks] should be slightly high.

Essential Teachings on Yue Wumu's Xingyiquan[21]

Essential Teaching One

IT HAS ALWAYS BEEN that what is scattered must have a gathering, what is divided must have a reuniting. Therefore, everywhere between Heaven and earth the multitudes all have their category. The chaotic thousand beginnings and the ten thousand endings all have their origins. Now one root fragmenting into ten thousand differences, and the ten thousand differences all returning to one root: this is an inevitable matter. Discussion of martial matters is also very complex, but the most important point is that amid the endless change, there is nothing that is not a posture, and nothing that is without qi. Although the postures are not the same, the qi returns to one. What is called "one" is everything—from the top of the head to the bottom of the feet; internally from the zang-fu organs, tendons, and bones externally to the muscles and the skin; the five sense organs; and everywhere—mutually connected and singularly united. Cleave it and it does not break; collide with it and it does not scatter. When above is about to move, below naturally follows it. When below is about to move, above naturally leads it. When above and below move, the center segment drives them. When the center segment moves, above and below harmonize with it. Internal and external are mutually connected, and front and back are mutually coordinated. That which is called singularly united is described thus, but this must not be sought forcefully; only by following the concept can it then happen. When still, be quiet and calm, fixed and stable like a mountain. When moving, be like thunder or like a cave-in, issuing forth quickly like lightning. When still, there is nothing that is not still; one is completely without unharmonious or worried intention outside, inside,

32

above, and below. When moving, there is nothing that does not move; the left and right, front and back, are joined without any restricted or wavering form. [When one is] authentic like water's free downward motion that nothing can block, and like fire's internal eruption that flares before one is able to cover one's ears, not fixated, [then] the thoughts are clear and unperturbed, the purpose sincere; and without expecting someting to be so, it will be so. Nothing causes it, but it manifests. How is it that it is without a source, but can be like this? Qi relies on the accumulation of days to have benefit, and skill relies on long practice to begin to form. Observing the teachings of the sages regarding [this] singular unity, it must wait until after the effort to extend [one's] knowledge through long listening and careful assessment from a broad perspective, and through unceasing investigation of phenomena, and then understanding matters will not be difficult. Skill can only be completed naturally, and one cannot skip levels and cannot hurry, but must advance sequentially step-by-step; and later the vessels and bones, limbs and joints, will naturally have a unity. When it is not difficult to connect above and below, outside and inside, so that the scattered is gathered and the divided is united, then everywhere within the four limbs finally will have returned to one singular qi.

Essential Teaching Two

Former generations did not discuss striking without simultaneously discussing qi. Qi at its most basic is unified, but can be divided into two. These two are called inhaling and exhaling. Inhaling and exhaling are yin and yang. Striking cannot exist without motion and stillness, and qi cannot exist without inhaling and exhaling. Inhaling is yin, exhaling is yang. What is based in stillness is yin; what is based in movement is yang. Ascending is yang, and descending is yin. Yang qi ascending upward is yang, whereas yang qi moving downward is yin. Yin qi moving downward is yin, whereas yin qi ascending upward is yang. These are the divisions of yin and yang. What are the clear and the turbid? That which ascends upward is clear; that which descends downward is turbid. Clear qi ascends upward; turbid qi descends downward. Clear is yang, turbid is yin, and yang is required to nourish yin. Discussing it as a whole, it is all qi. Discussing it in its parts, it is yin and yang. Qi cannot exist without yin and yang. When it is said that humans cannot exist without movement and stillness, the nose cannot be without inhaling and exhaling, and the mouth cannot be without intaking and expelling, this concerns the unchanging principle of circulation. Although the qi is divided into two, in actuality it is one. Those who have an interest in this direction should be careful to not take this as insignificant.

Essential Teaching Three

Qi is rooted in the body and in the segments of the body without a fixed position. The three segments are above, middle, and below. When speaking of the body, the head is the upper segment, the torso is the middle segment, and the legs are the lower segment. When speaking of the upper segment, the forehead is the upper segment, the nose is the middle segment, and the chin is the lower segment. When speaking of the middle segment, the chest is the upper segment, the abdomen is the middle segment, and the dantian is the lower segment. When speaking of the lower segment, the feet are the tip segment, the knees are the middle segment, and the hips are the root segment. When speaking of the arms, the hands are the tip segment, the elbows are the middle segment, and the shoulders are the root segment. When speaking of the hands, the fingers are the tip segment, the palms are the middle segment, and the heels of the palms are the root segment. Observing this, the feet do not need to be discussed. From the crown to the feet, there is nothing that does not have three segments. In short, if there is no division into three segments, then this is a place that does not manifest intention. If the upper segment is unclear, there is no responsiveness or purpose. If the middle segment is unclear, the entire body is empty. If the lower segment is unclear, one will experience stumbling or falling. Are these things that can be neglected? Regarding the actuation of qi, it must be that the tip segment moves, the middle segment follows, and the root segment initiates. However, this is still speaking of it divided segment by segment. If speaking of it as unified, then from the crown of the head to the bottoms of the feet and everywhere within the four limbs are always one segment, so how can there be three segments? And how within each of these three segments can there be three further segments?

Essential Teaching Four

In addition to discussing the body and qi, we must advance to discussing the termini. The termini are the body's tips. Those who talk about the body do not address these early on, and those who talk about qi rarely discuss them. Striking originates internally and is issued outward, the qi passing through the body and reaching the termini. Therefore, if the utilization of qi is not rooted in the body, then qi will be empty and insubstantial. If it does not manifest in the termini, then even when substantial, qi will still be empty. How can the termini not be explained? However, this specifically [refers to] the termini of the body, and still does not address the termini of the qi.

What are the four termini? Hair is the first. Everything associated with hair is not listed in the five elements, has no connection to the four limbs, and so seems unnecessary to discuss. However, hair is the terminus of the blood, and blood is the sea of qi. Even if it is not necessary to focus on the hair to discuss qi, we cannot depart from [the idea of] the blood giving rise to qi and, not leaving [this concept of the] blood, then we have no choice but to simultaneously discuss the hair, for if the hair is able to stand on end, then the blood terminus is sufficient. Another is the tongue, which is the terminus of the muscles. The muscles are the containers of qi. If the qi cannot form in the terminus of the muscles, then there is no ability to increase the capacity of qi. Therefore, the tongue must press the teeth, and then the muscle terminus will be full. The terminus of the bones is the teeth, and the terminus of the sinews is the nails. Qi originates in the bones and unites in the tendons. If [qi] does not reach the teeth, then it has not reached the terminus of the tendons. For those wishing to make qi ample, they cannot do it if the teeth do not influence the sinews, and if the nails do not reveal the bones. In the end, if one can be like this, then the four termini will be sufficient. If the four termini are sufficient, then the qi will also naturally be ample. And then how can one be empty and insubstantial, or substantial and yet still empty?

Essential Teaching Five

Now we use striking to discuss postures, and postures to discuss qi. Humans obtain the five zang organs to take form, and the five zang organs give rise to qi. If the five zang organs are full, they are the source of vitality, and are the root of creating qi; these are the heart, liver, spleen, lungs, and kidneys. The heart is fire, and has the image of flaring upward. The liver is wood, and has the form of crooked and straight. The spleen is earth, and has the power of solidity and abundance. The lungs are metal, and have the ability to follow and transform. The kidneys are water, and have the skill to moisten downward. These are the relationships of the five zang organs that must be harmonized with the qi, each according to its correspondence. Discussing all martial arts matters does not depart from this. The hollow of the chest is the location of the lung meridian, and is the canopy over all the zang organs. Therefore, if the lung meridian moves, then all the zang organs cannot be still. Between the two breasts lies the heart, guarded by the lungs, and below the lungs and above the stomach is the heart meridian. The heart is the sovereign fire; move and there is nothing that the ministerial fire does not nourish and unite. Between the two ribs on the left is the liver, and on the right is the spleen.[22] The fourteen segments of the spine[23] are all the kidneys, and these are the points for strengthening the five zang organs. The relations of the five [zang] organs are such that they all relate along the spine and connect to the kidney essence; therefore, they are also the kidneys. As to the waist, this is the original position of the two kidneys, and is the primary seat of the pre-Heaven and is especially the root source of all the zang organs. Therefore, if the kidney water is ample, then metal, wood, water, fire, and earth will all have vitality. These are the positions of the five zang organs. Now each of the five [zang] organs has its fixed position internally, and throughout the body also each has its specific correspondences. The neck, head, brain, bones, and spine are the kidneys. The two ears also are the kidneys. The two lips and two [lower] cheeks are the spleen. The two hairs[24] are the lungs. *Tianting*[25] is the vertex of the six yang meridians, gathers the essence of the five zang organs, and is actually the point on the head that governs the brain, and the whole body through the Governing Vessel. *Yintang*[26] is an important point for the stomach *yangming qi*. When the vitality of *tianting* is awakened, the mechanism reaches it through *yintang*. The qi produced from the kidneys reaching the six yang meridians is truly due to the key nature of *tianting*. The two eyes are the liver; but upon further examination, the upper eyelid is the spleen and the lower eyelid is the stomach, while the medial canthus is the heart meridian and the lateral canthus is the small intestine meridian. The sclera is the lungs, and the iris is the liver. The pupils of the eyes are the kidneys, and actually are the gathering of the essence of the five [zang] organs, and cannot be specifically called the liver. The nostrils are the lungs, and the two [upper] cheeks are the kidneys. The tragus is the gallbladder meridian, and behind the ears on the mastoid process is also the kidneys. The nose is central earth, the source of growth of the ten thousand things, and truly the governor of central qi. Within a person it is the meeting place of blood and qi, which both rush up to *yintang* and reach *tianting*, and it is also an extremely important area. Below the two lips is *chengjiang*,[27] and below *chengjiang* is the chin, which both correspond to *tianting* above, and are also the location of the kidney meridian. The neck is the pathway of the five [zang] organs and is the meeting place of qi and blood. In front is the passage for ingesting and expelling sustenance and qi, and in back is the route for kidney qi to ascend and descend. Liver qi travels through it moving to the left, and spleen qi travels through it moving to the right. This is an even more important relationship and is an important point for the whole body. The two breasts are the liver, the two shoulders are the lungs, and the two elbows are the kidneys. The four limbs are the spleen; the upper back and upper arms are all the spleen; and the ten fingers are the heart, liver, spleen, lungs, and kidneys. The knees and shins are the kidneys, the two heels are important parts of the kidneys, and *yongquan*[28] is a kidney point. In general, any places on the body that protrude relate to the heart; any that are sunken relate to the lungs. Places where the bones are revealed are the kidneys, places where the tendons connect are the liver, and places where the muscles are thick are the spleen. To give image to meaning, the heart is like a fierce tiger, the liver is like an arrow. Spleen qi and power are vast and inexhaustible. The location of the liver meridian is most unpredictably changeable. The movement of kidney qi is fast like the wind. These are the functions; but to utilize the meridians, taking any place on the body that corresponds to a certain meridian, in the end cannot be without intention. This will be felt in the body by practitioners, but cannot be expressed through brush and ink. As to creation, destruction, controlling, and transforming, although this is for discussion elsewhere, if one researches the required points they will naturally reach unification. The five elements and the hundred bodies will become as one source, and the four limbs and the three centers will harmonize as one qi. Why then must we understand from some individual meridian and discuss it in bits and pieces?

Essential Teaching Six

The mind harmonizes with the intention; the intention harmonizes with the qi; the qi harmonizes with the power: these are the three internal harmonies. The hands harmonize with the feet; the elbows harmonize with the knees; the shoulders harmonize with the hips: these are the three external harmonies. These together are called the six harmonies. The left hand harmonizes with the right foot; the left elbow harmonizes with the right knee; the left shoulder harmonizes with the right hip; and conversely so on the right side. The head harmonizes with the hands; the hands harmonize with the body; the body harmonizes with the footwork. Are these not also external harmonies?

The mind harmonizes with the eyes; the liver harmonizes with the tendons; the spleen harmonizes with the muscles; the lungs harmonize with the body; the kidneys harmonize with the bones. Are these not also internal harmonies? Are there then truly only six harmonies? Actually, these only describe the constituent parts. In the end, if one moves, then there are none that do not move; if one harmonizes, then there are none that do not harmonize. The five elements and the head, torso, and four limbs can be known from this.

Essential Teaching Seven

The head is the principal among the six yang meridians, and governs the entire being. Of the five sense organs and all parts of the body, there are none that do not rely on this. Therefore, the head must advance. The hands serve as the first to move, but the foundation is in the upper arm. If the upper arm does not advance, then the hands are lacking and do not advance. This is the importance of using the upper arm in advancing. The qi gathers at *zhongwan;* the mechanism is in the waist. If the waist does not advance, then the qi is spiritless and insubstantial. This is the importance of using the waist in advancing. The intention fills the entire body, and movement is in the footwork. If the footwork does not advance, then of course the intention cannot act. This is why the footwork must advance. Therefore, to step forward left, the right must advance; to step forward right, the left must advance. These are the seven advancings; how [can there be] any place that does not apply force? More importantly, before advancing, unite the whole body and do not have the slightest intention regarding advancing; but as soon as you are advancing, gather the entire body and be wholly without contradictory or wavering form.

Essential Teaching Eight

What is body method? Simply: lengthwise and crosswise, high and low, advancing and retreating, reversing and flanking. Lengthwise is releasing the power with one release and no rebound. Crosswise is wrapping [the opponent's] power, opening but not obstructing. High is raising the body as if increasing in stature. Low is restraining the body as if the form is gathering and contracting. When advancing, advance and destroy their body, bravely rushing in straight. When retreating, retreat leading their qi and spinning to a crouching posture. Regarding turning the body and blocking to the rear, the rear then becomes the front. Block laterally to the left and right, so that to the left and right none dare try to match you.[29] But this must not be carried out haphazardly. It is imperative to first observe a person's strengths and weaknesses and then to carry out one's strategy, utilizing sudden lengthwise movement and sudden crosswise movement. Lengthwise and crosswise change according to the force, and must not press on with only one ambition. Being suddenly high and then suddenly low, with high and low following the timing to shift, do not hold according to only one form. When it is time to advance, do not retreat and make the qi timid. When it is time to retreat, then initiate retreating with the form of advancing. Thus, advancing is advancing resolutely, and retreating actually also relies on advancing. If turning the body and blocking to the rear, block to the rear but also do not feel it is the rear. Block laterally to the left and right, but left and right also should not feel like left and right. In summary, strategize with the eyes, be flexible in adapting in the mind, and grasp the important points and establish them in the entire body. When the body goes forward, the four limbs are not commanded but still move; and when the body withdraws, there is not one of the constituent pieces that does not locate effortlessly. How can it be then that [these considerations of] body method can be presented but not discussed?

Essential Teaching Nine

All of the five sense organs and all parts of the body are governed by movement, but actually movement relies on stepping. Stepping is the foundation of the body and is the key to movement. Therefore, though accepting a challenge and facing an opponent all originates in the body, what is used to support the body in actuality is only the stepping. Following the opportunity and responding with change resides in the hands, but all of the transformations of the hands are also in the stepping. When advancing and retreating, reversing and flanking, without the footwork how can one create the opportunity to surge forth? When rising and falling, extending and contracting, without the stepping how can one demonstrate the miraculousness of change? What is described as "the strategy is in the eyes, and changeability lies in the mind," all of the twistings and turnings and endless changeability, and not being pressed and in danger—how is the fate of any of these not controlled by footwork? This must not be sought with force. Movement arises from no-mind; inspiration comes from the unconscious. When the body is about to move, the stepping carries it out. When the hands are about to move, the footwork impels them first without thinking, as if driven but not driven. What is called "above is about to move, and below naturally follows" is described thus. Steps are divided into front and back, with steps that have a fixed position and steps that are without a fixed position. If the front step advances and the back step follows, then front and back each has a fixed position. If the front step becomes the back, and the back step becomes the front—or even further, if taking a front step formed by the front step becoming the back, or if taking a back step formed by the back step becoming the front—then front and back are naturally without fixed positions. In sum, boxing utilizes discourse on postures, but the essentials are grasped in the stepping. Liveliness and sluggishness are in the stepping; agility and clumsiness are also in the stepping. The function of stepping is crucial.[30]

This boxing is called Mind Intention. Regarding mind intention, the intention is born from the mind, the fists follow the intention in movement, and one must always know the self and know the other person, following the opportunity and responding with change. When the mind's qi issues, then the four limbs all move. The feet lift, having a location; the knees lift, having an understanding; and movement and turning have a position. Unifying the arms and aiming with the hips, the three tips align, and internally the trio of mind, intention, and qi mutually harmonize. The fists harmonizing with the feet, the elbows harmonizing with the knees, and the shoulders harmonizing with the hips are the external trio mutually harmonizing. The three centers—the centers of the hands, the centers of the feet, and the center of the core—mutually harmonize with one qi. If far, then do not issue the hands; hit and strike inside of five feet and outside of three feet. Whether forward or backward, left or right, use as a standard: one step and one strike, issuing hands in order to reach the opponent, miraculously not exhibiting the form. Issue the hands quickly like wind and arrows, with a sound like thunder ringing, appearing and disappearing like a rabbit or a bird darting into the forest. Meet the enemy with the force of a great cannon collapsing a wall, the eyes bright, the hands quick, jumping straight forward and swallowing them. Before crossing hands, a unified qi stands in the vanguard, but after entering their hands, miraculousness lies in agile movement. Seeing an opening, do not strike; seeing their flank, strike. Seeing an opening, do not seize the position; seeing their flank, seize. Above, middle, and below, the qi is always composed, the body, feet, and hands regulated and controlled, not rising into emptiness and also not falling into emptiness, dexterous and clever, engaged wholly in liveliness, with the ability to go or stay, to be hard or soft, to advance or retreat. Not moving like a mountain, difficult to know like yin and yang, without exhaustion like Heaven and earth, full and ample like the imperial granary, vast and expansive like the four oceans, dazzling and glorious like the three lights. Observe the opportunity of incoming force, and assess the enemy's weakness and strength. Stillness used to handle movement contains an advancing method. Movement used to deal with stillness contains a borrowing method. Borrowing methods are easy, advancing methods are difficult, but advancing methods still should be foremost. When meeting one who is brave, do not contemplate mistakes. Those who contemplate mistakes take inch steps and find it difficult to move. Rise like an arrow drilling, and fall like the wind, one hand pulling and one hand attacking forward. Movements harmonize naturally in secret, rapidly like lightning in the heavens, striking and blocking to the two sides left and right, turning around like a tiger searching the mountains. Chop and strike bravely and fiercely so it cannot be stopped, chopping the tip, meeting the face, and seeking the central palace, stealing above and stealing below, the postures like a tiger or like an eagle or hawk descending on a chicken farm. Overturning the rivers and toppling the seas need not be hurried; a single phoenix facing the sun is already powerful. Behind the clouds, the sun and moon and Heaven and earth meet. When martial artists struggle, it manifests weak and strong. Step on the path one inch apart, and open the stance one foot. Split to the face and go, stepping forward with the right leg and advancing with the left step. This is the method for moving forward. To advance on others you must advance the body, the body and hands arriving together; only this is real. Issuing is decisive; what need is there to explain it? Understand the meaning and it is almost supernatural, like a hawk drilling through the forest without showing its wings, or an eagle seizing a small bird with power even in all directions. To snatch victory, the four termini must unite, but the foremost still must be the hands guarding the heart. The strategy is carried out with adaptability—suddenly, and with spirit. A cruel heart is considered the superior plan; then the hands and eyes can overcome others. What is dodging? What is advancing? Advancing is dodging, and dodging is advancing; it is not necessary to stray far to seek this. What is striking? What is blocking? Blocking is striking, and striking is blocking: simply issuing the hands. The mind is like gunpowder, and the hands like bullets; with a nimble flick of the trigger, the bird has difficulty in flying away. The body is like a bowstring, and the hands are like arrows. Aim the bow toward the bird, and it falls like a divine miracle. Raise the hands like lightning; lightning flashes too quickly to blink. Strike like sudden thunder; thunder claps too fast to cover the ears. The five methods at their core are five methods of sealing off. Without anyone to guard me, I block myself. The left hand passes, and the right hand goes out. The right hand goes past, and the left hand comes. The two hands clench as fists facing upward and issue. The defenses of the five senses must be strict. The fists issue from the heart and fall toward the tip of the nose. The foot rises from the ground, and when the foot rises quickly the heart fire has risen. Of the five elements—metal, wood, water, fire, and earth—fire flares upward and water moves downward. I have a heart, liver, spleen, lungs, and kidneys, and without a doubt the five elements mutually transform and evolve.

Methods for Crossing Hands[31]

Engage the right and advance left. Engage the left and advance right. When stepping, the heel touches the ground first, the tips of the feet use the ten toes to grasp the ground, the steps must be stable and the body must be solid. Striking must sink and be substantial and have bone power, commencing as a loose hand and becoming a fist when contacting the person. If using the fist it must clench tightly; if using the palm it must have qi. Above and below, the qi must be integrated and even. Entering and exiting use the heart as the commander; and the eyes, hands, and feet go forth following it, not deficient or lacking, not too close or too far away. The elbows sink and conceal, the hands sink and cover. The right foot moves first, the point of the upper arm facing forward; this is changing stepping. The fists issue from the heart using the power of the body to impel the hands, the hands guarding the heart and the heart controlling the hands. Advance the body and advance the steps, one strike with each step, and if one part moves all the parts follow. When issuing, there is decisiveness. When one grasps, the entire body grasps; when one extends, the entire body extends. Extending must extend advancing, and grasping must grasp viciously, like rolling a firecracker, which, when rolled tightly, explodes with force. Whether lifting striking, pressing striking, uprooting striking, spinning striking, chopping striking, thrusting striking, digging striking, elbow striking, arm striking, hip or palm striking, head striking, advancing-step striking, retreating-step striking, flowing-step striking, cross-step striking, forward, backward, left, right, above, below—all of the hundred types of striking methods must follow each other. When extending the hands, first engage the main gate. This is called cleverness. The joints must align. If they do not align, then there is no power. When the hands grasp, they must be agile; if not agile, then this gives rise to uncertainty. Issuing the hands must be fast; if not fast, then slow and incorrect. Raising the hands must be lively; if not lively, then not fast. Striking with the hands, one must follow; if not following, then not supplemented. The intent must be cruel; if not cruel, then wavering. The hands and feet must be lively; if not lively, then taking on danger. The intent must be complete; if not complete, then foolish. In action like an eagle grasping, brave and fierce, externally calm but with great nerve, the opportunity must be clearly utilized, completely without any fear or hesitation. The mind is small but the nerve is great, the countenance righteous but the heart evil. When still, like a scholar; when moving, like the sound of thunder. The incoming postures of others should be observed: When the feet kick does the head tilt? When the fists strike do the arms feint? Does the chest tighten when advancing? Does the body lean on [one] when issuing? Do they move obliquely to change stances? Do they fall backward when blocking and striking? When the legs are lifting do they overextend when issuing? The foot blocks pointing to the east, but should guard against slaughter from the west. If the first strike is empty, the second must be substantial. There are numerous ways to fall into the trap, thus the best methods come from careful contemplation. Hands that are quick beat hands that are slow; this common saying cannot be taken lightly, for it indeed is based on experience. Rise seeking to fall, and fall seeking to rise, as rising and falling repeatedly follow each other. When the body and hands arrive together, this is true. With scissor legs,[32] strike toward the eyebrows; and additionally turn around like a tiger searching the mountain. Raise the hands like lightning, strike downward like a thunderclap, the rain driving the wind, an eagle seizing a swallow, a sparrow hawk darting through the forest, a lion pouncing on a hare. When raising the hands, the three centers align. When not moving, be like a scholar. When moving, be like a dragon or a tiger. If distant, do not strike with the hands; keep the two hands guarding beside the heart. If the attack comes from the right, meet it with the right; if the attack comes from the left, meet it with the left. This is the fastest choice. If farther away lift the hands, and if close add the elbows. If farther away kick with the feet, and if close add the knees. Far and near should be known. The fists strike and the feet kick, but from the head to the stance, judge the opponent, with the ability to gather in one thought and advance. Have intention but do not exhibit the form. Exhibiting form must certainly not be victorious. The method for quickly dealing with someone is to carefully observe the environment, and strike with the fists from a superior position. The hands must be quick, the feet must be light, and the stances must move like a cat roaming. The mind must be centered, the eyes gather the spirit, and the hands and feet arrive, which must absolutely be victorious. If the hands arrive but stepping does not arrive, then striking others will not be miraculous. If the hands arrive and the stepping also arrives, then striking someone will be like mowing grass. Above strike the throat, below strike the groin, and if on the centerline strike the left and right ribs. Striking forward ten feet is not considered too far; but when close, strike only within the space of an inch. When the body moves, it is like toppling a wall. When the feet set down, it is like a tree sinking roots. The hands rise like cannonballs rushing straight out. The body must be like a live snake; strike at its head, and you will be attacked by its tail; strike at its tail, and you will be attacked by its head; strike at its middle, and you will be attacked by head and tail both.[33] Striking forward, one must attend to the rear. To know advancing, one must know retreating. The mind moves quickly like a horse; the arms move fast like the wind. When training, be as if someone is in front of your face; when crossing hands, although there is someone, act as if there is no one. Raise the front hand, and the rear hand presses closely. Lift the front foot, and the rear foot follows closely. When there is a hand in front of the face, do not see the hand; when there is an elbow in front of the chest, do not see the elbow. If seeing an opening, do not attack; if seeing an opening, do not advance. The fists do not strike rising into emptiness, and also do not strike falling into emptiness. When the hands rise, the feet must fall. When the feet fall, the hands must rise. The mind must take the lead, the intention must overcome the opponent, the body must attack the opponent, and the stepping must pass through the opponent, the front leg bent and the back leg stable. The head must look upward, the chest must expand upward, the waist must lengthen upward, and the dantian must transport qi. From the top of the head to the feet must be a singular, unified qi. If the courage is struggling and the heart is cold, one is absolutely not able to snatch victory. Those who are not able to judge the words and observe the color will absolutely not be able to defend against others, and definitely will not be able to move first. Whoever moves first is the master; whoever moves second is the student. If able to gather together as one thought to advance, then do not show [even] one thought of retreating. The three segments must integrate, the three tips must align, and the four termini must arrive together. Clearly understanding the three centers increases power. Clearly understanding the three segments increases the methods. Clearly understanding the four termini brings refinement. Clearly understanding the five elements increases qi. Clearly understanding the three segments and not being insufficient or lacking in rising and falling or advancing and retreating increases changeability. The three repetitions of nine turns[34] are one force, and always must have a unified mind as the commander. United in the five elements, conveyed in the two qi, drilled regularly without error, trained with effort morning and evening, the art and skill will naturally form over time. These words are sincere, and these phrases are not empty!

EXPLANATION OF THE FIVE FISTS

Required Knowledge for Practice

FIRST, TIME. In practicing Xingyiquan, it is best to undertake it at dawn, and the length of time must not be overly long, using one hour as a limit. For the sake of economizing on time, reducing this to thirty or forty minutes is also acceptable. Only one must not cease, and must practice daily; only in this way will there be benefit for the body. If, due to work concerns, there is no free time early in the morning, one can practice it at midday, or evening, or at several fixed times. Only after eating is it not appropriate; one should wait one or two hours, and then it is acceptable.

Second, space. The location should be inside, and an area fifteen feet long by eight feet wide is sufficient to undertake it. This is only talking about one person practicing in their home; if one will practice together with several people, then an appropriately sized location must be further determined.

Third, interspersed rest. Practice time commonly uses five minutes as a guide. Rest time also uses five minutes as a guide, meaning train until reaching five minutes' time, rest for five minutes, then practice again, and so on. Those whose body is strong and still have reserve energy, or whose strength is lacking and cannot continue for five minutes, must increase or decrease this according to the state of their individual vitality.

Fourth, prohibitions. When training inside, although one wants fresh air to circulate, one must not allow a strong wind to blow in, and one should close the windows on the side facing the wind. For example, if in winter the north wind is strong, then close the northern-facing window and open the southern-facing window. Xingyiquan cultivates the qi, enlivens the blood, lengthens power, and strengthens the tendons and bones; and, after practicing for several minutes when wet with sweat and when the hundred points are open, at this time if the wind blows then it is easy to suffer from cold invasion. Therefore, when resting during training, although one may become excited and hot, do not use a fan to seek wind, and after ceasing training one must wait until the body is warm and perspiration has stopped, and then may leave the training room. Also, during training time the heart and mind must be united. During these fixed times, one must not drink porridge, smoke, or eat any foodstuffs, and also must not banter loudly. When resting for five minutes during training, although the body feels tired, one must not sit. Instead, one should slowly walk around several times so the mind will be calmed and the strength will also recover. Thus, in a group training facility, do not arrange chairs. When practicing on summer days, do not, because it's hot, go bare-armed; the body must remain covered in wet clothing. When practicing on winter days, do not, because of the cold, wear so many clothes that one is ungainly and unable to move, but instead strip off outer jackets.

First Sequence—Splitting Fist

FUNCTIONS

Splitting Fist corresponds to metal, and is the rising and falling of a unified qi. Splitting uses the palm moving downward, like the splitting of an axe. Therefore, according to Five Element Theory it corresponds to metal, and its form is like an axe. Within the body it corresponds to the lungs, and in boxing it is splitting. If its energy is flowing, then the lung qi will be stable; if its energy is incorrect, then the lung qi will be abnormal. For humans, qi is the most crucial; if the qi is stable, then the body will be solid, but if the qi is abnormal, then the body will be weak. Therefore, Xingyiquan uses Splitting as its beginning, and cultivating qi as its first objective.

Preparatory Posture

Standing Erect. In Xingyiquan, the art of standing erect is called Taiji Posture, and is similar to the standing-erect postures of other common physical exercises. The head presses straight up, the eyes look level directly forward, the mouth is closed, and the tip of the tongue curls up to the palate. The chest protrudes slightly forward, the two shoulders are level, and the lower abdomen is withdrawn slightly. The two legs and two heels press together tightly, the two knees are extended straight, the tips of the two feet are opened obliquely to the left and right, forming a 65 degree V-shape.[35] The two arms hang straight, the two hands are opened but slightly bent, and the hearts of the palms are pressing the body with the five fingers held together, as in figure 1.

Post-Standing Method. From the Taiji Posture advancing to perform Three Bodies Posture, commonly referred to as the post-standing method, the movement sequence is as follows:

1. Both arms rise slowly to the left and right, the fingers opened slightly, with the hearts of the palms facing up, each forming a half-circle as they rise to the level of the chin, then turn the hearts of the palms down with the fingers pointing at each other, and from in front of the chin form a straight line, slowly pressing downward and stopping at the level of the lower abdomen. At this time, the tips of the fingers are touching, with the little fingers facing outward and the thumbs facing inward, the two arms having made a circular movement as in figure 2. When pausing, the posture is as in figure 3.

2. Pause momentarily, then make fists with both hands, twisting outward, causing the hearts of the palms to face upward, pressing in the same location. At the same time, squat down with the body, the two knees bending forward slightly, forming a horse-riding stance, the abdomen filling with qi, the two *kua*[36] locked tightly. The movements are as in figure 4, with the ending posture as in figure 5.

3. The left fist presses in place and does not move as the heart of the right fist faces inward and moves from the center of the chest up and forward at an angle. As the fist extends in front of the chest, the fist and the arm both twist slightly to the right, causing the little-finger side of the fist to face inward and the thumb side to face outward, the heart of the palm turned slightly to the right. The eyes look at the right fist, the right arm forming an arc with the fist at the height of the eyebrows, as in figure 6.

4. According to the dotted line in figure 7, move the left fist, with the heart of the palm facing inward, inside the right arm, extending diagonally upward to the right from in front of the chest, overlapping with the right fist, the right fist outside, the left fist inside, as in figure 8. After forming the posture in figure 8, the two wrists should twist rapidly, opening outward (at this time, the heart of the right palm faces left, and the heart of the left palm faces right). The left hand makes a pushing gesture as it splits toward the front, the heart of the palm facing forward and slightly to the right. The right hand makes a pulling gesture, pressing downward and stopping at the right of the lower abdomen, the heart of the palm facing down. At the same time, the left foot treads forward one step, the left knee forming a plumb line with the left heel, completing the posture shown in Figure 9. The left foot faces straight forward; the right foot is slightly turned, with the tip of the foot slanted toward the right front. From standing erect to this [position] is the preparatory posture that begins each sequence in Xingyiquan.

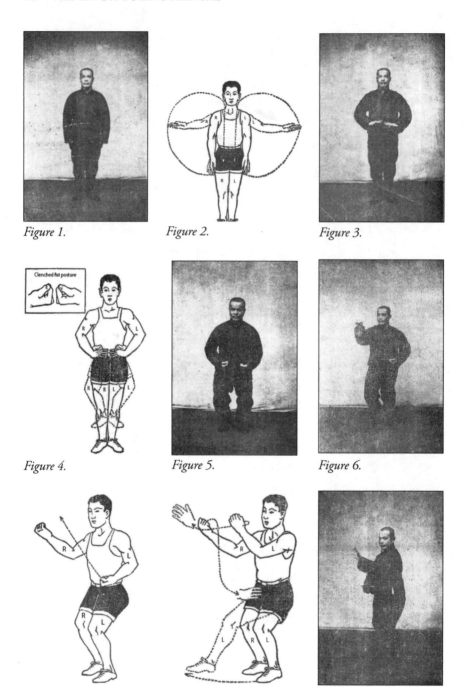

Figure 1.

Figure 2.

Figure 3.

Figure 4.

Figure 5.

Figure 6.

Figure 7.

Figure 8.

Figure 9.

Preparatory Posture Corrections. Xingyiquan's main efficacy is in training the qi. Thus, when standing erect, one must first close the mouth, clench the teeth, curl the tip of the tongue up to the palate, and inhale and exhale using the nose. Only while resting after completing one or several sequences should one start to again open the mouth. Closing the mouth ensures that the qi will not leak out, and simultaneously prevents inhalation of unclean air. The reason for this is that when breathing during training, although the breaths are more short and rapid than normal, the lungs will be open and this is the easiest time to inhale microbes. The tongue curling to the palate is so that the *jinye* fluids are produced. When jinye fluids are produced and swallowed, this causes the mouth to not be dry.

Also, when standing erect, the head must press upward, the neck must be straight, the chest must broaden, and the anus must lift, and only then will the posture be united.

In figure 5, after the legs are bent, the lower back must lift and the upper body must be straight. If bent forward or leaning back, everything will be full of errors.

In figure 8, the movements of the hands and feet must rise and fall together and cannot be uneven. The twisting of the wrists, the outward splitting of the left hand, and the downward pressing of the right hand all especially emphasize agility and naturalness.

Aside from this, four points should be most strongly heeded. In Xingyiquan, regardless of which fist is being trained, pay attention to these four points. The first is called wrapping the elbows; the second is called dropping the shoulders; the third is called inflating the belly; and the fourth is called expanding the chest.

Wrapping the elbows means, regardless of whether drilling upward or extending straight, the arms must be slightly bent, and then the power of the shoulders can move through them and be transported to the hands.

Dropping the shoulders causes the qi to not be floating, and thus to gather below in the lower abdomen.

Inflating the belly is receiving qi in the lower abdomen. The places that store qi in the body are the lungs and the lower abdomen. To store qi in the lungs, one must exhale out and then inhale the fresh qi anew; this qi cannot be stored long term. Qi stored in the lower abdomen does not require inhalation and exhalation and, compared to the qi in the lungs, can be maintained for a long time.

Expanding the chest causes the chest cavity to be open and broad, and aids respiration. When desiring to store qi in the lower abdomen, one must first depress the chest until flat, to force the lung qi to enter the dantian. However, in this way the lungs will then be constricted and the respiration cannot be free and fast. Therefore, one must also expand the chest, allowing the lungs to not obstruct the respiration.

Post standing is also called yin-yang post standing, and can be divided into high and low. When first beginning practice, one should use a high stance and wait until there is a foundation, then switch to a low stance. If one is able to first stand well in this post, practice of all of the other fists will naturally be easy.

THE STEPPING PATTERN OF SPLITTING FIST

The stepping pattern of Splitting Fist is carried out along a straight line. In figure 10, from L/R to L1 is the stepping pattern of the preparatory posture. L1 with a half-step becomes L2, and the right then advances a step, changing to R3. At the same time, the right hand splits forth, forming a right Splitting Fist. R3 with a half-step becomes R4, and L2 then advances a step, changing to L5. At the same time, the left hand splits forth, forming a left Splitting Fist. Continue to advance as shown. Figure 11 is the stepping pattern for turning toward the right rear, and figure 12 is the stepping pattern for turning toward the left rear.

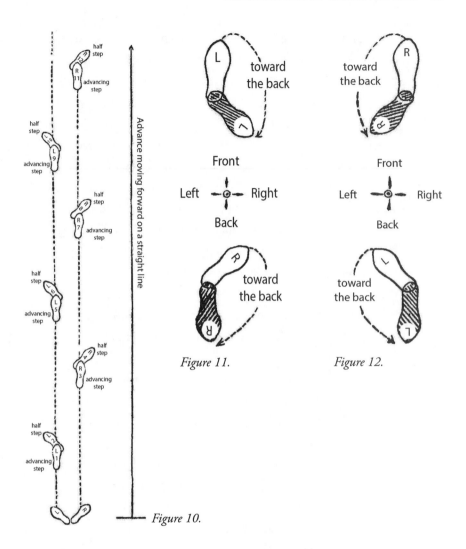

Figure 11.

Figure 12.

Figure 10.

THE MOVEMENTS OF SPLITTING FIST

Right Splitting. Figure 13 is the preparatory posture, which is a left Splitting Fist.

1. Desiring to move from a left Splitting posture to a right Splitting posture, according to the dotted lines in figure 13, first make a fist with the left hand and from the front position pull back and downward, facing in, describing a large circle,

and again extending upward from the chest, striking out in the same place as before. As the left hand pulls back, the five fingers first should slightly curl, then with power make a pulling motion, first becoming a fist when reaching the side of the abdomen. When reaching the chest, further twist the arm to the left, causing the heart of the palm to face left (see the dotted line in front of the chest in figure 13) while issuing obliquely forward and up. Thus, after striking outward, the thumb will face outward and the little finger will face inward, with the heart of the palm inclined toward the left. At the same time, as in figure 14, the left foot steps forward, angled to the left (the step should be small, perhaps six inches), called a half-step.

2. After completing the posture in figure 14 according to the dotted lines in that figure, the right hand twists upward and becomes a fist, the heart of the palm facing up, forming a small circle and issuing obliquely from the chest toward the upper left, overlapping with the left fist, the heart of the left palm facing left, the heart of the right palm facing right. At this time, the right foot already has the intention of stepping forward, but is still pressing down and has not moved, as in figure 15.

3. According to the dotted lines in figure 15, at the same time the right wrist twists to the left, release the fist in a pushing posture, splitting toward the front, at the height of the brow. The left wrist twists to the right, releasing the fist in a pulling-back posture, pressing down until reaching the left side of the abdomen, and then stops, the heart of the palm facing down. At the same time, the right foot takes a step forward (the step should be large and advance straight like an arrow), causing the right knee to form a plumb line with the right heel. This is called an advancing step, and forms a right Splitting posture, as in figure 16.

The movements of right Splitting in 1–3 at their core are continuous, and the rising and falling of the two arms is carried out simultaneously, without differentiating between first and second. However, within this book, in order to allow the reader to clearly understand and to think carefully, it is necessary to divide this into a sequence and arrange the explanation through illustrations. Students should feel this intention within their bodies, and it is imperative that their movements not be as restricted and sluggish as in the illustrations. For everything that follows, this is the same.

Figure 13.   Figure 14.   Figure 15.

Figure 16.

Left Splitting. The movements of left Splitting and right Splitting on the whole have no great differences. It is simply that movements of the right hand and right foot are changed to using the left hand and left foot, and the movements of the left hand and left foot are changed to using the right hand and right foot. Learning one and drawing inferences, students can seek left Splitting from within all of the movements of right Splitting.

1. Figure 17 is a right Splitting posture. According to the dotted lines in the figure, make a fist with the right hand, and from the front position pull back and downward, facing in, describing a large circle, and again extending upward from the chest, striking out in the same place as before. As the right hand pulls back, the five fingers should slightly curl, and with power make a pulling motion, first becoming a fist when reaching the side of the abdomen. When reaching the chest, further twist the arm to the right, causing the heart of the palm to face right while issuing obliquely forward and up. Thus, after striking outward, the thumb will face outward and the little finger will face inward, with the heart of the palm inclined toward the right. At the same time, as in figure 18, the right foot steps forward, angled to the right (the step should be small, perhaps six inches), called a half-step.

2. According to the dotted lines in figure 18, the left hand twists upward and becomes a fist, the heart of the palm facing up, forming a small circle and issuing obliquely from the chest toward the upper right, overlapping with the left fist, the heart of the right palm facing right, the heart of the left palm facing left. At this time, the left foot already has the intention of stepping forward, but is still pressing down and has not moved, as in figure 19.

3. According to the dotted lines in figure 19, at the same time the left wrist twists to the right, release the fist in a pushing posture splitting toward the front, at the height of the brow

and in line with the heart. The right wrist twists to the left, releasing the fist in a pulling-back posture, pressing down until reaching the right side of the abdomen, and then stops, the heart of the palm facing down. At the same time, the left foot takes a step forward (the step should be large and advance straight like an arrow), causing the left knee to form a plumb line with the left heel. This is called an advancing step, and forms a left Splitting posture, as in figure 20.

Figure 17.   *Figure 18.*   *Figure 19.*

Figure 20.

Left and Right Alternating Advancing. From the preparatory posture moving until reaching right Splitting, and from right Splitting to left Splitting, alternate advancing forward until one end of the room is reached and you cannot continue, turn to the rear and continue training until reaching a suitable time, then rest.

Turning to the Rear. Turning to the rear is divided into turning left and turning right. If turning to the rear from a left Splitting posture, one should turn toward the right rear. If turning to the rear from a right Splitting posture, then one should turn toward the left rear.

Turning to the Right Rear. Turning to the right rear is turning to the rear from a left Splitting posture.

1. According to the dotted lines in figure 21, from the front position the left hand pulls back and downward facing in, forming a half-circle. Reaching the left edge of the waist it stops, becoming a fist as the wrist twists toward the left, causing the heart of the palm to face upward. The right hand becomes a fist and twists toward the right, also causing the heart of the palm to face up, until it stops at the right edge of the waist. The two hands should move at the same time. Simultaneously, the two feet (left in front, right in back) both apply force with the heels to turn backward to the right, as in figure 22 (see figure 11 as a reference), thus having changed direction.

2. According to the dotted lines in figure 22, the right fist issues obliquely forward and up from the chest, and at the same time the right foot steps forward a small step angled to the right (a half-step), forming the posture in figure 23.

3. According to the dotted lines in figure 23, the left fist strikes forward and up to the right, overlapping with the right hand. At this time, the left foot already has the intention of stepping forward, but is still pressing down and has not moved, as in the

posture in figure 24. Although the orientation of the images is reversed, this posture is the same as in figure 19, and the movements are no different. Following the explanation of movements for figure 19, form a left Splitting Fist, as in figure 25.

Figure 21.   Figure 22.   Figure 23.

Figure 24.   Figure 25.

Turning to the Left Rear. Turning to the left rear is turning to the rear from a right Splitting posture.

1. According to the dotted lines in figure 26, from the front position the right hand pulls back, downward, and facing in, forming a half-circle. Reaching the right edge of the waist it stops, becoming a fist as the wrist twists toward the right, causing the heart of the palm to face upward. The left hand becomes a fist and twists toward the left, also causing the heart of the palm to face up, until it stops at the left edge of the waist. The two hands should move at the same time. Simultaneously, the two feet both apply force with the heels to turn backward to the left, as in figure 27 (see figure 12 as a reference), thus having changed direction.

2. According to the dotted lines in figure 27, the left fist issues obliquely forward and up from the chest, and at the same time the left foot steps forward a small step angled to the left (a half-step), forming the posture in figure 28.

3. According to the dotted lines in figure 28, the right fist strikes forward and up to the left, overlapping with the left fist. At this time, the right foot already has the intention of stepping forward, but is still pressing down and has not moved, as in the posture in figure 29. Although the orientation of the images is reversed, this posture is the same as in figure 15, and the movements are no different. Following the explanation of movements for figure 15, form a right Splitting Fist, as in figure 30.

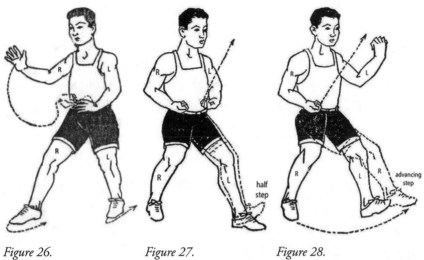

Figure 26.   Figure 27.   Figure 28.

Figure 29.   Figure 30.

Considerations for Ending Practice

Regardless of which boxing sequence is being trained, when an appropriate length of time has been reached and practice ends, one should hold whatever posture is being trained for one minute, paying attention to any places of error and correcting them. For example, if practicing Splitting Fist and ending in a left Splitting posture, then remain in that left Splitting posture.

Correcting and Adjusting Postures

Hand position. Regardless of whether it is the hand positions of left Splitting posture or right Splitting posture, the fingers of both hands all spread open, the thumb level horizontally, the index finger extending forward, the tiger's mouth forming the shape of a half-circle, and all the joints of the fingers should be curved. The two eyes together should watch the tiger's mouth of the hand splitting forward.

Shoulder position. The shoulders should hook inward, and their energy must sink downward in a relaxed way.

Elbow and knee position. The elbow of the hand that splits outward should be aligned and form a straight line with the knee and cannot be disjointed. The elbow of the hand pulling backward and down should wrap tightly to the waist. (This is the same for each of the sequences below.)

Arm position. During any movement, the arms should make an arc shape, and must not form an evident angle. It is correct only if they seem straight but are not straight, seem bent but are not bent.

The Rhyme Song of Splitting Fist

The two hands issue from the mouth,
drilling up and out at the level of the brow,
the back fist following closely.
The arms embrace the ribs at the level of the heart,
the *qi* follows the body's movements and sinks to the *dantian,*
as the two hands fall together and the back foot follows.

The fingers are spread, and the tiger's mouth round,
the front arm is at the height of the heart,
the back hand is hidden beneath the ribs.
The tips of the hand, foot, and nose are all in a line,
the small finger is turned up at the level of the brow.
The striking method of Splitting Fist is to drill up.
As the feet and hands fall, the tip of the tongue pushes up.
Step forward to change postures and the *yin* hand drops.

Second Sequence—Drilling Fist

FUNCTIONS

Drilling Fist corresponds to water, and the movement of its qi is like the winding and twisting of water; there is nowhere it does not flow to. Within the body it corresponds to the kidneys, and in boxing it is drilling. If following the principles when practicing, then the qi is harmonious and the kidneys are full. If not following the principles when practicing, then the qi is disturbed and the kidneys are empty. If the qi is disturbed and the kidneys are empty, then the clear qi cannot ascend and the turbid qi cannot descend, and the true power of this fist cannot be issued. Students should know this.

PREPARATORY POSTURE

The same as for Splitting Fist (movements in figures 1–9).

THE STEPPING PATTERN OF DRILLING FIST

The stepping and turning patterns for Drilling Fist are exactly the same as for Splitting Fist. Therefore, the explanations for figures 31–33 are the same as those for figures 10–12.

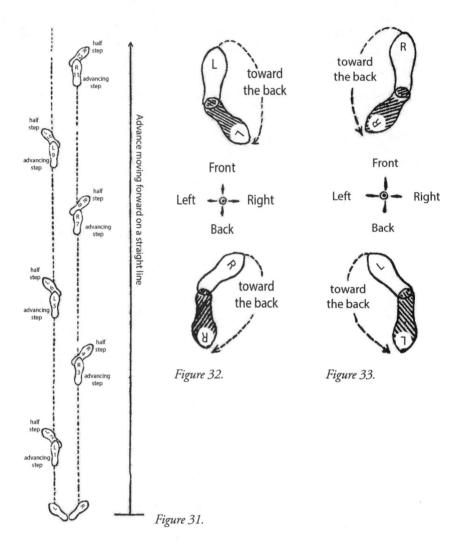

Figure 32.

Figure 33.

Figure 31.

THE MOVEMENTS OF DRILLING FIST

Right Drilling

1. From the preparatory posture, according to the dotted lines in figure 34, simultaneously the left hand forms a half-circle, from the front position pulling back downward, facing inward and slightly to the right, as the right hand becomes a fist, twisting outward, causing the heart of the palm to face

upward, and issues obliquely up and forward from in front of the chest. At this time, the hearts of the palms already face inward, as in figure 35. As the left hand pulls back, reaching position L2, and the right hand strikes out, reaching position R2 (at this time the right fist follows along the left arm pressing, and furthermore should strike upward from inside the left arm), the left foot advances a half-step forward, angled to the left, forming the posture in figure 35.

2. According to the dotted lines in figure 35, following closely on the movements of figure 34 and without slowing in between, the left hand clenches into a fist and pulls from L2 to L3 at the left edge of the waist, the heart of the palm facing down, as the right hand continues from R2 and issues obliquely upward, reaching R3, and then stops. At the same time, the right foot advances forward with a large step, causing the right knee to form a plumb line with the right heel, forming a right Drilling posture, as in figure 36.

Figure 34.

Figure 35.

Figure 36.

Left Drilling. The difference between left Drilling and right Drilling is only that the movements of the left and right hands and feet are switched. Therefore, if one has already studied right Drilling, the movements of left Drilling can be sought from this.

1. Figure 37 is a right Drilling posture. Desiring to move from right Drilling to left Drilling, according to the dotted lines in figure 37, the right hand opens and the wrist twists to the left (if changing from left Drilling to right Drilling, the left hand opens and the wrist twists to the right) and from the front position pulls back downward and slightly to the left, facing in, forming a half-circle. The left hand becomes a fist, twisting outward causing the heart of the palm to face up, and issues obliquely forward and up from in front of the chest. As the right hand pulls back, reaching position R2, the left hand strikes out, reaching position L2. At this time, the left fist follows the left arm, pressing together, and the left fist must strike upward from inside the right arm. The right foot then advances a half-step forward, angled to the right, forming the posture in figure 38.

2. According to the dotted lines in figure 38, both hands continue to move and, following closely on the movements of figure 37, and without slowing in between, the right hand forms a fist and retracts from R2 to R3 at the right edge of the waist, the heart of the palm facing down. The left fist continues from L2 and issues obliquely upward, reaching L3, and then stops. At the same time, the left foot advances forward with a large step, causing the left knee to form a plumb line with the left heel, forming a left Drilling posture, as in figure 39.

Figure 37.   *Figure 38.*   *Figure 39.*

Left and Right Alternating Advancing. From the preparatory posture practicing until reaching right Drilling, and from right Drilling to left Drilling, alternate advancing forward until one end of the room is reached and you cannot continue, turn to the rear and continue training until reaching a suitable time, then rest.

Turning to the Rear. Turning to the rear is divided into turning left and turning right. If turning to the rear from a left Drilling posture, one should turn toward the right rear. If turning to the rear from a right Drilling posture, one should turn toward the left rear.

Turning to the Right Rear. Turning to the right rear is turning to the rear from a left Drilling posture.

1. According to the dotted lines in figure 40, from the front position the left fist pulls back downward and facing in, forming a half-circle, until reaching the left edge of the waist, the left wrist twisting left, causing the heart of the palm to face up. The right fist twists toward the right in its original position, also causing the heart of the palm to face up. The two hands must move at the same time. Simultaneously, the two feet

(left in front, right in back) both use the heel to apply force and turn backward to the right, as in figure 41 (see figure 32 for reference), thus having changed direction.

2. According to the dotted lines in figure 41, the right fist issues obliquely forward and up from in front of the chest, and at the same time the right foot steps forward a small step angled to the right (a half-step), forming the posture in figure 42.

3. According to the dotted lines in figure 42, the heart of the left fist faces inward as it strikes obliquely forward and up from in front of the chest. The right fist opens as the right wrist twists toward the left, and from the front position pulls back downward, facing inward and slightly to the left, reaching the right edge of the waist as in R3, and stops. Simultaneously, the left foot advances forward a large step, again forming a left Drilling posture, as in figure 43.

Figure 40.   Figure 41.   Figure 42.

Figure 43.

Turning to the Left Rear. Turning to the left rear is turning to the rear from a right Drilling posture.

1. According to the dotted lines in figure 44, from the front position the right fist pulls back downward and facing in, forming a half-circle, until reaching the right edge of the waist, the right wrist twisting toward the right, causing the heart of the palm to face up. The left wrist twists toward the left in its original position, also causing the heart of the palm to face up. The two hands must move at the same time. Simultaneously, the two feet (right in front, left in back) both use the heel to apply force and turn backward to the left, as in figure 45 (see figure 33 for reference), thus having changed direction.

2. According to the dotted lines in figure 45, the left fist issues obliquely forward and up from in front of the chest, and at the same time the left foot steps forward a small step angled to the left (a half-step), forming the posture in figure 46.

3. According to the dotted lines in figure 46, the heart of the right fist faces inward as it strikes obliquely forward and up

from in front of the chest. The left fist opens as the left wrist twists toward the right, and from the front position pulls back downward and slightly to the right, facing inward, reaching the left edge of the waist as in L3, and stops. At the same time, the right foot advances forward a large step, again forming a right Drilling posture, as in figure 47.

Figure 44.   Figure 45.   Figure 46.

Figure 47.

Considerations for Ending Practice

The same as for Splitting Fist.

Correcting and Adjusting Postures

The posture for Drilling Fist is almost the same as for Splitting Fist, but there are two points that should most strictly be paid attention to, described as follows:

First, the movements of the half-steps and advancing steps of Drilling Fist must be lively, and not like those of Splitting Fist, which can be slightly relaxed. As one fist of Drilling Fist extends upward and the other fist pulls back, one foot takes a half-step. When the two hands overlap in front of the chest, the half-step is already completed and the other foot must then advance. Only in this way can the movements of the hands and feet then be coordinated and not disorganized.

Second, when one fist is pulling back downward and one fist is extending upward, the fist extending upward must drill forth inside and above the arm of the fist being pulled back. Only then is the posture unified. Also, the upward-drilling fist is at the height of the brow, the thumb facing outward, the little finger facing inward, while the backward-pulling fist presses down at the side of the abdomen, the heart of the palm facing down (left Drilling pressing at the left side of the abdomen, right Drilling pressing at the right side of the abdomen). When drilling forth, the little finger also must turn upward and the eyes must focus on the fist.

The Rhyme Song of Drilling Fist

The front *yin* hand hooks downward,
the rear *yang* hand drills upward.
When issuing, drill high at the level of the brow.
The two elbows hug the heart as the back foot rises,
the eyes watch the front hand as the four extremities stop.
When Drilling Fist changes postures, the body moves,

the front foot steps first, the back foot follows,
the back *yin* palm is hidden beneath the elbow.
When setting the foot down, the three points must always align.
The front *yang* hand strikes the tip of the nose,
the little finger turns up, the elbow guards the heart.
The advancing step of Drilling Fist also strikes the tip of the nose,
the front palm hooks with the wrist and crosses downward;
advance as the palms turn, and the striking fist extends.

Third Sequence—Smashing Fist

FUNCTIONS

Smashing Fist corresponds to wood, and the coming and going of the two hands is like arrows issuing or like stringing pearls, thus it is the expansion and contraction of a unified qi. Within the body it corresponds to the liver, and in boxing it is smashing. Training and obtaining its methods can calm the qi and smooth the liver, increase the spirit, strengthen the tendons and bones, and bolster mental acuity. Its benefits are not meager.

PREPARATORY POSTURE

The same as for Splitting Fist (movements in figures 1–9).

THE STEPPING PATTERN OF SMASHING FIST

The stepping pattern of Smashing Fist, aside from the preparatory posture, is carried out along a straight line, first an advancing step and second a following step, as in figure 48. The advancing steps are all with the left foot, and the following steps are all with the right foot. Its method is very simple, and learning it is quite easy. Only the stepping pattern when turning to the rear, because the right foot must lift in the air, is somewhat difficult to learn. Figure 49 is the stepping pattern for turning toward the right rear.

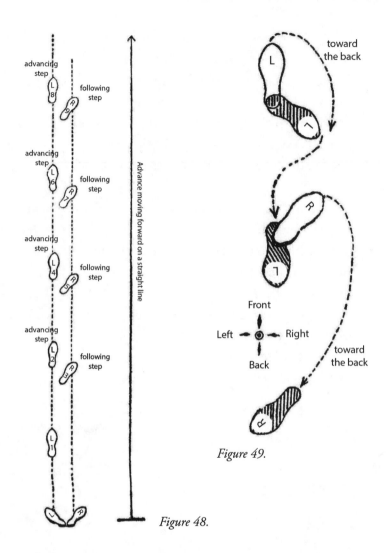

Figure 48.

Figure 49.

THE MOVEMENTS OF SMASHING FIST

Right Smashing. The preparatory posture in figure 50 is the same as in figure 9. Smashing Fist is like the stretching of a bow. The arm that extends forward is like pressing the arrow, and the arm bent behind is like pulling the bowstring. The stepping pattern does not change; only the arms extending and contracting differentiate left and right. Extending the left arm is called left Smashing; extending the right arm is called right Smashing.

1. According to the dotted lines in figure 50, the left hand becomes a fist and extends forward, the heart of the palm facing right. The right hand becomes a fist and twists outward, causing the heart of the palm to face up, as in figure 51.

2. According to the dotted lines in figure 51, the left elbow bends backward as the left hand draws back, causing the heart of the palm to face upward, fixing at the left edge of the waist. The right fist twists left, causing the heart of the palm to face left, and issues forward level. The elbow should be slightly bent and cannot be too straight, the fist level with the center of the chest, and the thumb tilted slightly forward. The two hands should move together at the same time. Simultaneously, the left foot advances a step with the tip of the foot straight forward, and the right foot follows a step, the tip of the foot angled to the right. When following, the foot does not rise high and should advance grazing the ground. This forms a right Smashing Fist, as in figure 52.

Figure 50.   *Figure 51.*   *Figure 52.*

Left Smashing. The stepping pattern of left Smashing is the same as the stepping pattern of right Smashing; only the movements of the coming and going of the fists are reversed.

1. Figure 53 is a right Smashing posture. According to the dotted lines in the figure, the right elbow bends backward as the right fist draws back, causing the heart of the palm to face upward, fixing at the right edge of the waist. The left fist twists right, causing the heart of the palm to face right, and issues forward level. The elbow should be slightly bent and should not be too straight, the fist level with the center of the chest, and the thumb tilted slightly forward. The two hands should move together at the same time. Simultaneously, the left foot advances a step, with the tip of the foot straight forward, and the right foot follows a step, with the tip of the foot angled to the right. When following, the foot does not rise high and should advance grazing the ground. This forms a left Smashing Fist, as in figure 54.

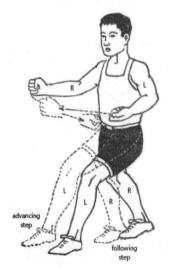

Figure 53.   *Figure 54.*

Left and Right Alternating Advancing. From the preparatory posture, practice until reaching right Smashing, and from right Smashing to left Smashing, alternate advancing forward until one end of the room is reached and you cannot continue, turn to the rear and continue training until reaching a suitable time, then rest.

Turning to the Rear. Turning to the rear in Smashing Fist originally had only one method. Because the hand positions of left Smashing and right Smashing are slightly different, now this is explained differentiating between left Smashing turning to the rear and right Smashing turning to the rear.

Left Smashing Turning to the Rear

1. Figure 55 is a left Smashing posture. According to the dotted lines in the figure, the left fist twists right, causing the heart of the palm to face downward, and from the front pulls downward facing in, pulling back until past the left side of the body, forming a half-circle, then the wrist again turns to the left, causing the heart of the palm to face upward, overturning and moving forward until stopping at the left side of the waist. The heart of the right palm faces inward and issues obliquely forward and up from the center of the chest, similar to a right Drilling posture. At the same time, the left heel applies force and turns to the right rear, the right foot lifts in the air, the tip of the foot facing right, the heel facing left, perpendicular to the forward direction, approximately one foot high, now having turned completely to the right rear, as in figure 56.

2. According to the dotted lines in figure 56, with the heart of the palm facing inward, the left fist issues obliquely up and right, inside the right arm and in front of the chest, overlapping with the right fist, as in figure 57. This must be closely followed by the movements below without pausing.

3. According to the dotted lines in figure 57, the two wrists twist rapidly and the two fists open up. At this time, the heart of the right palm faces left, and the heart of the left palm faces right. The left hand makes a pushing posture, splitting to the front, the heart of the palm forward and slightly right. The right hand makes a pulling-back posture, the heart of the palm facing downward, pressing downward until reaching the right side of the abdomen, and then stops. At the same time, the right foot sets down forward, treading where the dotted line indicates, the tip of the foot angled slightly to the right. The left foot follows, the tip of the foot turned slightly to the left, as in figure 58.

4. According to the dotted lines in figure 58, the left hand becomes a fist and extends forward, the heart of the palm facing right. The right hand becomes a fist, twisting outward, causing the heart of the palm to face upward, forming the posture in figure 59.

5. Figure 59 is the same [in mirror image] as figure 52. Moving [on the opposite sides] according to the dotted lines in that figure will again form a right Smashing posture, as in figure 60.

Figure 55.   *Figure 56.*   *Figure 57.*

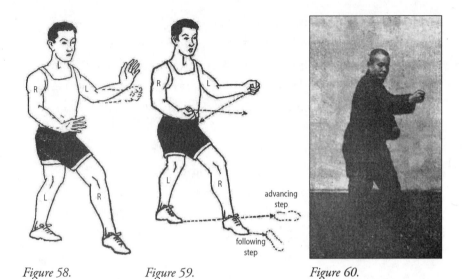

Figure 58.   Figure 59.   Figure 60.

Right Smashing Turning to the Rear

1. Figure 61 is a right Smashing posture. According to the dotted
   lines in the figure, the right fist twists left, causing the heart of
   the palm to face downward, and from the front pulls downward facing in, pulling back until past the right side of the
   body, forming a half-circle, then the wrist again turns to the
   right, causing the heart of the palm to face upward, overturning and moving forward with a small circular movement, then
   issuing obliquely forward and up from the center of the chest,
   similar to a right Drilling posture. At this time, the fist's movement, together with the first half-circle, has already formed
   an oval shape. Simultaneously, the left heel applies force and
   turns to the right rear, the right foot lifts in the air, the tip of
   the foot facing right, the heel facing left, perpendicular to the
   forward direction, approximately one foot high, now having
   turned completely to the right rear, as in figure 62.

2. The posture in figure 62 is the same as the posture in figure 56.
   The movements are the same as described in that figure.

3. The posture in figure 63 is the same as the posture in figure 57. The movements are the same as described in that figure.

4. The posture in figure 64 is the same as the posture in figure 58. The movements are the same as described in that figure.

5. The posture in figure 65 is the same as the posture in figure 59. The movements are the same as described in that figure.

6. The posture in figure 66 is the same as the posture in figure 60, which is a right Smashing posture.

Figure 61.   Figure 62.   Figure 63.

Figure 64.   Figure 65.   Figure 66.

Closing Posture. When ceasing Smashing Fist, there is a special closing stance that is dissimilar from the closing stance of other sequences. Figure 67 is a right Smashing posture. The Smashing Fist closing posture must be performed after reaching a right Smashing posture; otherwise, the force will not flow. Students must especially pay attention to this.

1. According to the dotted lines in figure 67, the right foot first takes a small step back, forming the posture in figure 68.

2. According to the dotted lines in figure 68, the right elbow bends backward as the right fist draws back, causing the heart of the palm to face upward and fix at the right edge of the waist. The left fist twists right, causing the heart of the palm to face right, issuing forward level. The movements of the two hands are the same as in figure 53. At the same time, the left foot takes a large step back, as in figure 69.

3. According to the dotted lines in figure 69, the left fist twists right, causing the heart of the palm to face downward, and from front position draws back downward, stopping when arriving between the hips in front of the left leg. At this time, the heart of the palm is already facing inward. At the same time as the left fist moves, the right fist twists to the left, also causing the heart of the palm to face downward, pressing downward from the lower abdomen, stopping when arriving between the hips in front of the right leg. The heart of the palm faces inward, at the same height as the left fist. Simultaneously, the left foot steps forward and slightly to the right, describing an arc shape, the right heel applies force and causes the tip of the foot to twist right, and both knees bend, forming an angle of about 60 degrees, but with the waist and back upright, forming the Smashing Fist closing posture, as in figures 70A (rear view) and 70B (front view).

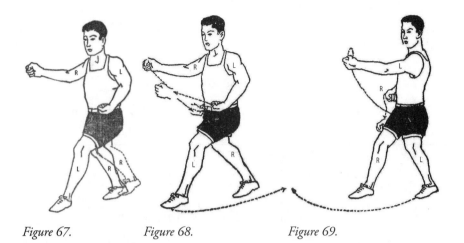

Figure 67.   *Figure 68.*   *Figure 69.*

Figure 70A.   *Figure 70B.*

Considerations for Ending Practice

The same as for Splitting Fist.

Correcting and Adjusting Postures

With the stepping pattern for Smashing Fist, the front foot should not hook inward and cannot turn outward. The rear foot should seem straight but not be straight, seem turned but not be turned.

The hand positions should be such that the hands do not leave the heart, and the elbows do not leave the ribs.

The extension and contraction of the two arms and the advancing and retreating of the two feet require rising together and falling together, and cannot have even the slightest concatenation.

The elbow of the arm that extends forward should have downward sinking energy, and the elbow bending backward should have pulling energy. The shoulders are relaxed and open; the eyes look forward at the middle joint of the index finger of the extended hand.

The fist that pulls back, whether left or right, should press tightly against the ribs on either side of the heart. The hand that extends is at the height of the heart.

The Rhyme Song of Smashing Fist

In the Smashing Fist posture, the three tips align,
the tiger's eye[37] faces up, at the level of the heart.
The back *yang* hand is hidden beneath the ribs.
The front foot must be straight, the back foot turned.
The back foot must be stable, making a V-shape.
When Smashing Fist turns, reach the height of the brow,
the body stands straight and true as the foot is lifted,
the foot is raised, then strikes out horizontally below the knee,
the foot and hand fall together into scissor legs,[38]
the front foot turned, the back foot straight.

The striking method of Smashing Fist is to push the tip of the
    tongue up,
rub and extend above the elbow of the front hand,
advance and issue, first striking the ribs,
the back foot following closely.

Fourth Sequence—Pounding Fist

FUNCTIONS

Pounding Fist corresponds to fire, and is the opening and closing of a unified qi. Like the flash explosion of a cannon, with its projectile issuing
suddenly, its nature is most violent, and its form is most fierce. Within the
body, it corresponds to the heart, and in boxing it is pounding. When practicing according to its methods, the body will be at ease and the qi harmonious. If not practicing according to its methods, then the limbs will not be
fluid and the qi will be disturbed. If the qi is harmonious, then the mind is
empty and luminous. If the qi is disturbed, then the mind is muddled and
confused. Students must deeply research this.

PREPARATORY POSTURE

The same as for Splitting Fist (movements in figures 1–9).

THE STEPPING PATTERN OF POUNDING FIST

Aside from the stepping of the preparatory posture, which is similar to that
of all other sequences, the stepping pattern of Pounding Fist follows a saw-
tooth line in advancing forward, as in figure 71. The stepping methods are
divided into four types: The first is called half-step, and is stepping maneu-
vering to the left or right, used in forming a crooked line. Second is lifting
step, where the foot lifts into the air and does not touch the ground. Third
is called advancing step, and fourth is following step. Advancing steps are
straight, and following steps form slight oblique angles. These are the four

main stepping patterns of Pounding Fist. Turning to the rear is also divided into the two methods of turning to the left and turning to the right, as in figures 72 and 73.

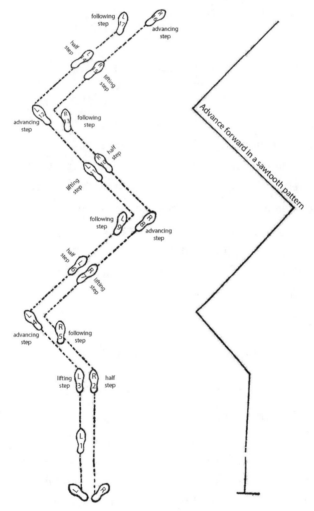

Figure 71.

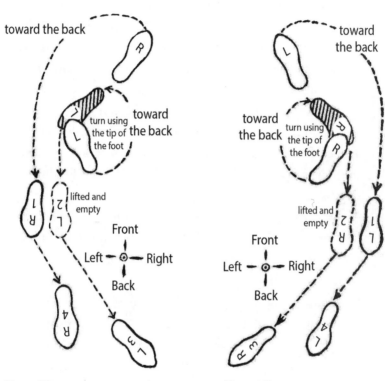

Figure 72.   Figure 73.

THE MOVEMENTS OF POUNDING FIST

Right Pounding

1. Figure 74 is the preparatory posture. According to the dotted lines in the figure, both hands extend forward level, the hearts of the palms facing downward, at the height of the center of the chest, making a pulling movement toward the front. At the same time, the left foot advances forward a step (advancing step), and the right foot follows forward, reaching the inner shin of the left leg (the foot does not stop or touch the ground), and again treads forward a step (a half-step). The left foot then quickly rises and follows forward, reaching the inner shin of the right leg and lifting. This is called lifting step, as shown in figures 75 and 76.

2. According to the dotted lines in figure 76, from the front position the two hands pull back toward the body, both becoming fists as the left wrist twists to the left and the right wrist twists to the right, causing the hearts of both palms to face upward, stopping at the fold of the waist, as in figure 77.

3. According to the dotted lines in figure 77, the left fist twists inward, causing the heart of the palm to face downward, and overturns upward from the waist, forming an arcing line, reaching the left edge of the forehead, and stops, the heart of the palm facing forward. The right fist twists left and issues forward level, causing the heart of the palm to face left, the thumb slightly inclined forward, similar to the forward extension of Smashing Fist. At the same time, the left foot (the lifted foot) advances a step obliquely to the left front (advancing step), and the right foot (the half-stepping foot) follows forward a step, forming a right Pounding posture, as in figure 78.

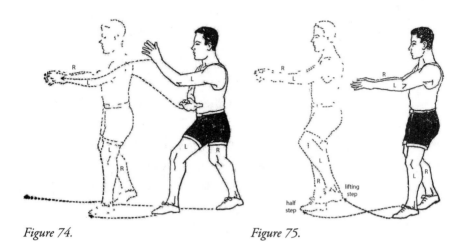

Figure 74.   Figure 75.

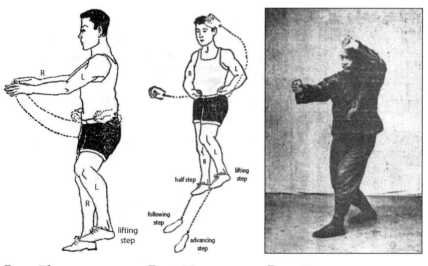

Figure 76.   Figure 77.   Figure 78.

Left Pounding. Left Pounding is the left fist extending forward and the right foot advancing forward, exactly the opposite of right Pounding's right fist and left foot forward. If carefully feeling this in the body, one may know one but infer many: the method of left Pounding can be sought from within right Pounding.

1. Figure 79 is a right Pounding posture. According to the dotted lines in the figure, from the left edge of the forehead toward the left front, the left fist pulls downward and back, forming a half-circle, until reaching the edge of the waist, causing the heart of the palm to face upward. The right fist pulls downward and back, toward the right side, also forming a small half-circle, until reaching the edge of the waist, causing the heart of the palm to face upward. At the same time, the left foot advances a step obliquely to the right front (half-step), and the right foot follows forward, reaching the inner shin of the left leg and lifting, as in figure 80.

2. According to the dotted lines in figure 80, the right fist twists inward, causing the heart of the palm to face downward, and overturns upward from the waist, forming an arcing line, reaching the right edge of the forehead, and stops, the heart of the palm facing forward. The left fist twists right and issues forward level, causing the heart of the palm to face right, the thumb slightly inclined forward, similar to the forward extension of Smashing Fist. At the same time, the right foot (the lifted foot) advances a step obliquely to the right front (advancing step), and the left foot (the half-stepping foot) follows forward a step, forming a left Pounding posture, as in figure 81.

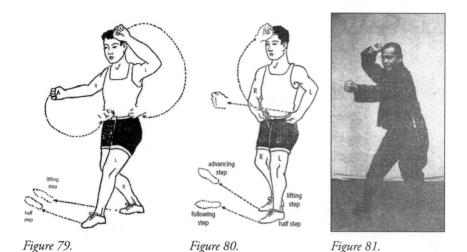

Figure 79.   Figure 80.   Figure 81.

Left and Right Alternating Advancing. From the preparatory posture, practice until reaching right Pounding, and from right Pounding to left Pounding, alternate advancing forward until one end of the room is reached and you cannot continue, turn to the rear and continue training until reaching a suitable time, then rest.

Turning to the Rear. Turning to the rear is divided into turning left and turning right. If turning to the rear from a left Pounding posture, one must turn left. If turning to the rear from a right Pounding posture, one must turn right.

Turning to the Left Rear. Figure 82 is a left Pounding posture. According to the dotted lines in the figure, from the right edge of the forehead toward the right front, the right fist pulls downward and back, forming a half-circle, until reaching the edge of the waist, causing the heart of the palm to face upward. The left fist pulls downward and back, toward the left side, also forming a small half-circle, until reaching the edge of the waist, causing the heart of the palm to face upward. At the same time, the tip of the left foot applies force and turns toward the left rear. The right foot lifts up and, brushing the ground and following the left foot toward the rear, sets down in a half-step (like the original foot position in the opposite direction).

The left foot again advances a step, tightly pressing the right inside shin and lifting (lifting step), forming the posture in figure 83 and having already turned toward the rear. See figure 72. The posture in figure 83 is the same as the posture in figure 77. Following the dotted lines and instructions for figure 77 again forms a right Pounding stance, as in figure 84.

Turning to the Right Rear. Figure 85 is a right Pounding posture. According to the dotted lines in the figure, from the left edge of the forehead toward the left front, the left fist pulls downward and back, forming a half-circle, until reaching the edge of the waist, causing the heart of the palm to face upward. The right fist pulls downward and back, toward the right side, also forming a small half-circle, until reaching the edge of the waist, causing the heart of the palm to face upward. At the same time, the tip of the right foot applies force and turns toward the right rear. The left foot lifts up and, brushing the ground and following the right toward the rear, sets down in a half-step (like the original foot position in the opposite direction). The right foot again advances a step, tightly pressing the left inside shin and lifting (lifting step), forming the posture in figure 86 and having already turned toward the rear. See figure 73. The posture in figure 86 is the same as the posture in figure 80. Following the dotted lines and instructions for figure 80 again forms a left Pounding stance, as in figure 87.

Figure 82.   *Figure 83.*   *Figure 84.*

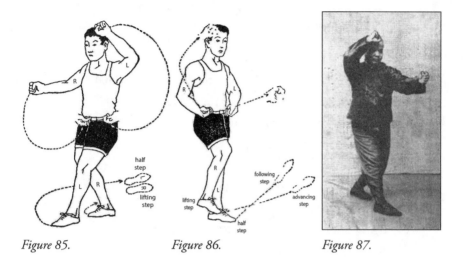

Figure 85.   *Figure 86.*   *Figure 87.*

Considerations for Ending Practice

The same as for Splitting Fist.

Correcting and Adjusting Postures

For the movements of Pounding Fist, the left hand should be connected with the left foot, the right hand should be connected with the right foot, and the left and right hands should especially be connected to the right and left feet, rising together and falling together.

The chest must open and expand, the lower abdomen must sink, the anus must lift, and the buttocks must not be stuck out.

Pounding Fist values emptiness within. Therefore, the two shoulders should be relaxed and open with pulling power.

For the fist drilling at the forehead, the elbow should sink downward; only then will it have trained power.

In right Pounding, the body should be turned toward the left; and in left Pounding, the body should be turned toward the right.

The Rhyme Song of Pounding Fist

The two elbows gather closely as the foot lifts up,
the two hands move together like a *yang* fist,
the front hand moves transversely, the back hand straight,
the two fists gather at the level of the navel,
the *qi* follows the body's movements and enters the *dantian*.
When the feet and hands fall together, the three tips align.
The fist strikes at the height of the heart,
the tiger's eye of the front hand presses up,
the back fist drills up at the height of the brow,
the tiger's eye faces down, and the elbow sinks.
The striking method of Pounding Fist is to lift the foot;
as the foot sets down, the front fist drills up.
The hands and feet fall together in a crossing step,[39]
the back foot following closely.

Fifth Sequence—Crossing Fist

FUNCTIONS

Crossing Fist corresponds to earth, and is the gathering of a unified qi. Within the body it corresponds to the spleen, and in boxing it is crossing. Its qi must flow. If flowing, then the spleen and stomach will be relaxed; if not, then the spleen and stomach will be empty and weak. In addition, the fist must unite the stance. If united, then the internal five elements will be united and the hundred parts of the body will be at ease. If incorrect, then the internal qi will lose harmony, and movements will all be chaotic. It must always be that the disposition is solid, the qi is flowing, the form is rounded, and the energy is harmonized; only then can one perfect the abilities of Crossing Fist. This is as the former philosophers said: "In the principles it is trustworthiness; in the body it is the spleen; in boxing it corresponds to crossing."

Preparatory Posture

The same as for Splitting Fist (movements in figures 1–9).

The Stepping Pattern of Crossing Fist

The stepping pattern of Crossing Fist advances forward following an undulating line, as in figure 88. The stepping methods are divided into three types: the first is called a half-step (also called turning step); the second is called advancing step; and the third is called following step. Turning to the rear also has two methods of turning to the left and turning to the right, as in figures 89 and 90.

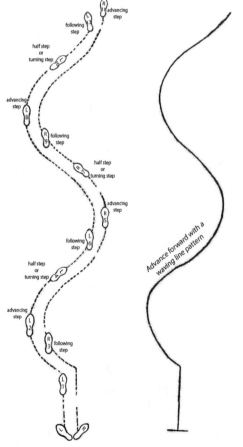

Figure 88.

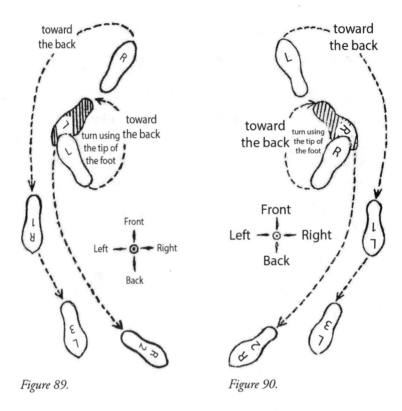

Figure 89.   Figure 90.

The Movements of Crossing Fist

Right Crossing

1. Figure 91 is the preparatory posture. According to the dotted lines in the figure, the left hand becomes a fist and twists toward the rear, causing the heart of the palm to face inward. At the same time, the right hand also becomes a fist and presses in its original position like Drilling Fist, forming the posture in figure 92.

2. According to the dotted lines in figure 92, the left fist twists to the right, from the forward position pulling back downward and facing in, bringing the forearm transversely in front of the abdomen, the heart of the palm facing down. The right fist twists outward, causing the heart of the palm to

face upward, issuing obliquely forward and up from in front of the chest. When moving, the two hands must move at the same time, and the right fist must extend forward and up in front of the left arm, unlike in right Drilling, where the right fist extends up and forward inside the left arm. At the same time, the left foot advances forward a step, forming an arc slightly toward the right (advancing step). The right foot follows forward a step (following step), the right knee of the following leg pressing tightly against the bend of the knee of the left leg, forming a right Crossing posture, as in figure 93.

Figure 91.   Figure 92.   Figure 93.

Left Crossing. Left Crossing is carried out from right Crossing, and the posture is the same as right Crossing, except that the left and right movements of the hands and feet are reversed.

1. Figure 94 is a right Crossing posture. According to the dotted lines in the figure, the left foot advances a step to the right front, forming a small arc shape; this is called a half-step, or a turning step, as in figure 95.

2. According to the dotted lines in figure 95, the right fist twists toward the left, from the forward position pulling back downward and facing in, bringing the forearm transversely in front of the abdomen, the heart of the palm facing down. The left fist twists outward, causing the heart of the palm to face upward, issuing obliquely forward and up from in front of the chest. When moving, the two hands must move at the same time, and the left fist must extend forward and up in front of the right arm, unlike in left Drilling, where the left fist extends up and forward inside the right arm. At the same time, the right foot advances forward a step, forming an arc slightly toward the left (advancing step). The left foot follows forward a step (following step), the left knee of the following leg pressing tightly against the bend of the knee of the right leg, forming a left Crossing posture, as in figure 96.

3. Figure 97 is a left Crossing stance. According to the dotted lines in the figure, the right foot advances a step to the left front, forming a small arc shape; this is called a half-step, or a turning step, as in figure 98.

4. The movements shown by the dotted lines in figure 98 are the same as in figure 92. At the moment the two hands move, the left foot advances forward a step, forming an arc slightly toward the right (advancing step). The right foot follows forward a step (following step), the right knee of the following leg pressing tightly against the bend of the knee of the left leg, forming a right Crossing posture, as in figure 99.

Figure 94.

Figure 95.

Figure 96.

Figure 97.

Figure 98.

Figure 99.

Left and Right Alternating Advancing. From the preparatory posture practicing until reaching right Crossing, and from right Crossing to left Crossing, alternate advancing forward until one end of the room is reached and you cannot continue, turn to the rear and continue training until reaching a suitable time, then rest.

Turning to the Rear. Crossing Fist turning to the rear is also divided into turning left and turning right. If turning from a left Crossing posture, then one should turn left. If turning from a right Crossing posture, then one should turn right.

Turning to the Left Rear

1. Figure 100 is a left Crossing posture. According to the dotted lines in the figure, the tip of the left foot applies force and turns toward the left rear. The right foot lifts up and, brushing the ground and following the left toward the rear, sets down as in figure 101.

2. The movements of the two hands shown by the dotted lines in figure 101 are the same as in figure 92, except that the left foot must advance a step toward the left front, forming an arc shape (advancing step). This is different from the advancing step in figure 98, which moves forward to the right. The right foot follows a step (following step), again forming a right Crossing posture, as in figure 102.

Turning to the Right Rear

1. Figure 103 is a right Crossing posture. According to the dotted lines in the figure, the tip of the right foot applies force and turns toward the right rear. The left foot lifts up and, brushing the ground and following the right toward the rear, sets down as in figure 104.

2. The movements of the two hands shown by the dotted lines in figure 104 are the same as in figure 95, except that the right foot must advance a step toward the right front, forming an

arc shape (advancing step). This is different from the advancing step in figure 95, which moves forward. The left foot follows a step (following step), again forming a left Crossing posture, as in figure 105.

Figure 100.   Figure 101.   Figure 102.

Figure 103.   Figure 104.   Figure 105.

Considerations for Ending Practice

The same as for Splitting Fist.

Correcting and Adjusting Postures

In left Crossing the body must twist toward the right, and in right Crossing the body must twist toward the left. The head, waist, fist, and foot must be connected just like a twisted rope.

When settling into a Crossing Fist stepping pattern, the knee of the back leg should press slightly against the curve of the knee of the front leg; only then can the posture be stable.

The movements of Crossing Fist are somewhat similar to those of Drilling Fist, except that in Drilling Fist the fist drills forth from inside the enclosure of the other arm, whereas Crossing Fist should drill forth outside the enclosure of the other arm.

In applying power, Crossing Fist values naturalness. As when tearing silk thread, one must apply force discreetly, without any trace of strenuously going too far.

The Rhyme Song of Crossing Fist

The front hand is *yang,* the back hand is *yin,*
the back hand is hidden beneath the elbow.
In changing postures and issuing, the foot rises up,
the body method is to stand unified so the *qi* can circulate,
the tip of the tongue curls up and the *qi* issues forth.
Crossing Fist changes postures with scissor legs,[40]
angle the body with the step, then the foot and hands fall,
the rear hand turns to *yang* and pulls out.
When setting the foot down, the *yang* hand and three tips align,
the tip of the nose and the tip of the foot follow closely.
The striking method of Crossing Fist makes the back fist *yin,*
the front is *yang,* and its elbow protects the heart.

Draw the bow to the left and right, pulling to the outside;
when the feet and hands fall together, the tip of the tongue curls.

Xingyiquan Summary Rhyme[41]

The three pressings:
The head presses upward, like pressing the ceiling.
The tongue presses upward, pressing against the palate.
The hands press outward, pressing as if upholding.
Clearly understanding the three pressings brings power to uproot
   trees.

The three hookings:
The head must hook downward, the eyes looking forward.
The edges of the shoulders must hook for the hands to exemplify
   naturalness.
The lower back must hook, and the feet must be connected.
The backs of the palms must hook.
The soles of the feet must hook downward.
Clearly understanding the three hookings increases spirit.

The three roundings:
The spine must round.
The shoulders and back must half-round as if arcing.
The chest must round, so the *qi* is naturally extended.
The tiger's mouth must round like a crescent.
Clearly understanding the three roundings transmits the subtlety.

The three holdings:
The *dantian* must hold *qi* as the root.
The mind must hold the body as its focus.

The arms must hold the integration of the four limbs.
Clearly understanding the three holdings brings movement.
Clearly understanding the three holdings can save one's life.

The three fallings:
The *qi* falls to the *dantian* for the body to be the principal.
The *qi* falls to the *dantian* so sickness will not arise.
The edges of the shoulders fall so the intention is pure.
The edges of the shoulders fall so deep intention is maintained.
The elbows fall for the shoulders to be the root.
Clearly understanding the three fallings makes the body clever.

The three arcings:
The arms must arc like a bow.
The wrists must arc pressing outward.
The legs must curve in a connected arc.
Clearly understanding the three arcings brings power.
Clearly understanding the three arcings, the postures are not lacking.

The three integrations:
The neck must be integrated in a vertical direction.
The head and neck must be integrated vertically without leaning.
The body method must be integrated to differentiate the four
    directions.
The legs and knees must be integrated below like the roots of a tree.
Clearly understanding the three integrations brings ability.
Clearly understanding the three integrations makes the skill
    profound.

Though the seven body methods are divided three by seven, the
    twenty-one methods are all one method.

When studying boxing one must only develop essential *qi*;
One must not develop hard *qi*.

AFTERWORD BY SHENG LINHUAI

I HAVE HAD A simple interest in Xingyi, but until now I have never pursued it. Fourth nephew Zecheng sought Yunting's art and brought him to Shanghai. In only a few months, followers thronged his doors, and fourth nephew was elated. Now all comrades and gentlemen throughout the world may benefit from these pictures and descriptions. In appreciation of Instructor Yunting's guidance, I attach this colophon.

Autumn, *guihai* year [1923]
Sheng Linhuai (盛麟懷) of Wujin

BIOGRAPHIES

E XCEPT FOR JIN YUNTING's own biography, taken from the 1930 edition, the biographies on the following pages are translated from the *Encyclopedia of Chinese Martial Arts,* published in 1998. Included here are all the main figures in Jin Yunting's Xingyi lineage beginning with the purported originator Yue Fei, with the exception of Li Kuiyuan, for whom no entry exists. These biographies are presented "as is," with all quotations and parenthetical notes following the original format. Obvious errata have been left unaltered, but footnoted where possible. Though ostensibly designed to serve as authoritative biographies, the *Encyclopedia* lists no sources for the facts and quotations therein, and no methodology for the collection of data. For now, readers should seek to compare these with the various other existing biographies, until more energy can be devoted to compiling thoroughly researched histories of these figures.—*Translator*

Biography of Yue Fei 岳飛

(1103–1142) Famous Song Dynasty anti-Jin general and people's hero. Courtesy name Pengju (鵬舉). Originally from Tangyin in Xiangzhou (present-day Tangyin County, Henan Province). His family was extremely poor, and as a youth he worked with his father doing farmwork by day and then studying by night, not sleeping until the late hours. He was fond of reading *Master Zuo's Spring and Autumn Annals* and admired Sun Wu's *Art of War.*

Even as a young man Yue Fei was full of integrity and possessed a heart blooming with "the promise of loyalty and righteousness to country." Under the military leader Zhou Tong and famous spearman Chen Guang, he studied and attained the essentials of martial arts and deployment of troops. When not yet an adult, Yue could already draw a 300-*jin*[42] bow and eight-*dan*[43] crossbow, and was skilled in the arts of archery and spear. He could shoot left- and right-handed; his martial arts skills exceeded all others; and he was "without peer in the county."

At the end of the Northern Song Dynasty, beginning when Yue was nineteen, he enlisted in the military four times. The first time he was the "Captain of ten squads" but resigned upon his father's death. Later, he became a Chariot-Brigade Commander and with determination led his troops into enemy territory, where they encountered a large enemy force and were scattered, forcing him to return home alone. During a high tide of national defense, he enlisted for the third time. Due to his skilled organization of remote pacification troops and his abilities in arms, he received a promotion to Trusted Gentleman. Later, because he met the enemy on the frozen battlefield and soundly defeated the Jin army, Yue was promoted to Gentleman Consultant, a lower-ranking military officer.

At the beginning of the second year of the *Jingkang* reign period (1127), under the leadership of Vice-Marshal Zong Ze, Yue was victorious against Jin troops many times. At the battle of Caozhou (northwest of present-day Cao County, Shandong Province) Yue took the lead in attacking the enemy troops, again soundly defeating the Jin army, this time chasing them for many miles in their retreat and cutting down still more of their soldiers. In deploying troops, Yue Fei advocated that "the cleverness of implementation is contained in one's mind," and that, after sizing up the situation and seizing the opportunity to move cleverly, "if the troops are skilled, and the general strong, then you can use one to stop ten." He was praised by Zong Ze, who proclaimed: "You are brave, wise, and talented, and are unsurpassed by even the great generals of old."

In the same year, the Emperors Huizong and Qinzong were kidnapped, and Zhao Gou seized the opportunity to ascend the throne as Gaozong. Gaozong did not heed the opposition of many of his ministers, relying only on the capitulationists, and moved the capital to Yangzhou, later establishing a new capital at Lin'an (present-day Hangzhou, Zhejiang Province). Yue Fei was by nature honest and straightforward, and wholly devoted to saving the common people. Although his position was low, and his words carried little weight, he still wrote an appeal to the emperor. In several thousand words he strongly requested to retake Bianjing (present-day Kaifeng, Henan Province) and regain Henan, and he resolutely opposed the court's retreat to the south. In the end, because of his "inappropriate words beyond the duties of a minor official," Yue was removed from his post. Because of his strong desire to serve his country, he thereupon sought the assistance of the patriot general Zhang Suo, Bandit-Suppression Commissioner of Hebei Province, who appointed Yue as a commander in the central army and later promoted him to Commander-General, a mid-level military officer. Yue was stern and careful in governing his army and viewed martial training and the strict pursuit of refinement and skill as the keys to the employment of troops. Because of this, there was not a battle that his "Yue Family troops" did not win. In the midst of one fierce battle, he seized the great Jin banner, personally captured the Jin general Tuobayewu, and stabbed to death the Jin Commander Heifengdawang. During the battle to guard Bianjing, he shot his bow with his left hand while wielding a lance in his right, crisscrossing through the enemy troops, who were thrown into great chaos and soundly defeated. When the Jin army caught wind of him, they would lose their resolve and exclaim in sorrow, "To move a mountain is easy; to move the Yue army is difficult."

Yue personally took part in 120 battles, and his fighting skill was awe-inspiring. His grandson Yue He said:

> My forefather observed "three strictnesses" in governing his army. First, he strictly controlled his forces. He valued selectiveness, once using five hundred of his best soldiers to defeat Wu Shu's fifty-thousand-man Jin army. He also was cautious in training, and between battles took every chance to train his troops, wearing heavy armor to scale walls and cross moats just as in actual battle. He was fair in reward and punishment; when his adopted son Yue Yun did not take training seriously and his horse subsequently lost its front shoe, Yue Fei assigned him

one hundred lashes as punishment. He created clear command signals that were simple and readily apparent, so that when the signal was issued, his orders were carried out. He observed strict discipline, stating that he would "freeze to death before breaking into houses (not forcing his troops into people's homes), starve to death before plundering and seizing." He set himself as the example, never committing even the smallest infraction. He ate and bivouacked together with his soldiers, sharing their same fortunes and misfortunes. When a soldier was injured, he would personally mix medicine for him. If a soldier sacrificed himself, he would provide for his surviving relatives. Rewards were handed out to all, and he did not keep any for himself.

Second, he strictly controlled his household. He considered farming and study his primary concerns. He did not seek to take advantage of others' power and influence, and did not seek personal gain and positions. If his son performed a military feat, he would not petition for reward and would refuse any that was offered. His residence was thrifty and frugal, he wore only simple clothes and seldom ate meat, and he restrained himself, striving for filial piety and adherence to the Dao, never forgetting his mother's training to "serve the country with true sincerity."

Third, he strictly controlled himself. He did not covet wealth nor put aside farming. He was not attached to lust and kept a household without concubines. He did not brag, and he used his land to support the destitute families of deceased soldiers and his poorer relatives.

The Emperor rewarded Yue Fei with military landholdings and would not accept his request to retire, believing that "if scholar-ministers do not love money, and martial-ministers do not pity death, then all is right in the world." He was successively conferred with the titles of Military Revenues Commissioner of the Army for Frontier Pacification, Dynasty-Founding

Marquis of Wuchang Commandery, Junior Guardian, Defender-in-Chief, and Bandit-Suppression Commissioner of the North and South.

In the ninth year of the *Shaoxing* reign period (1139) Gaozong, fearing the Jin, willingly "moved to the left of the river" and with the traitorous minister Qin Kuai strongly advocated for peace negotiations with the Jin. Yue Fei again submitted a petition fiercely opposing this. The next year, the great Jin army led by Wu Shu attacked Henan. Yue Fei again led his soldiers in counterattack, greatly defeating the Jin army at the cities of Yan and Yingchang (present-day Xuchang, Henan Province), and recaptured Zhengzhou and Luoyang. He then led his troops to Zhuxian township, with his vanguard drawing near Bianjing and continuously pounding toward the enemy's center. Hearing of this, the people's militia of the two rivers rose up to join him. At this time, Gaozong and Qin Kuai, with treacherous hearts, bent to the Jin demand that "Yue Fei must die in order to sign a treaty" and, surprisingly, in one day sent twelve golden tablets (imperial edicts) instructing him to retreat.

Yue Fei dejectedly returned to Lin'an, and that night he was stripped of his military powers and given the new title Vice-Commissioner of Military Affairs. Not long after, he was framed for plotting rebellion and imprisoned. Preferring death to capitulation, he stopped eating. In the eleventh year of the *Shaoxing* reign period, on the twenty-ninth of the twelfth lunar month (January 27, 1142), on baseless and false charges, Yue Fei, his adopted son Yue Yun, and his General-Assistant Zhang Xuan were executed. As he drew near the execution ground, he wrote on his deposition, "One day Heaven will vindicate me! One day Heaven will vindicate me!"

Twenty years later, Xiaozong Zhao Shen assumed the throne and, in order to calm the anger of the people, encouraged soldiers to resist the enemy and finally settled Yue Fei's unjust sentence. His body was exhumed and reburied according to proper rite in Xixialingluan in Hangzhou, with his son Yue Yun at his side. The burial plot was named the "Garden of Essential Loyalty." In the sixth year of the *Qiandao* reign period (1170) the "Loyal Exemplars Temple" was built in his honor in Ezhou (present-day

Wuchang, Hubei Province). In the sixth year of the *Chunxi* reign period (1179) Yue was posthumously named Wumu (武穆), and in the fourth year of Ningzong's J*iatai* reign period (1204) he was posthumously granted the title Prince of E [Ezhou, above]. In the first year of Lizong's *Baoqing* reign period [1225], Yue's posthumous name was changed to Zhongwu (忠武) and *Prince Yue Zhongwu's Posthumously Collected Writings* was published. His poems and essays were impassioned and filled with the strong feelings of love of country. His representative work, the ode "The Whole River Is Red," is a passionate, rousing work that shines as bright as the sun and moon.

According to legend, the martial arts creations by Yue Fei include Yue-style Connected Boxing, *The Xingyi Boxing Manual,* Yue-style Boxing (ten sets), Yue-style Spear, Hooked Spear, Double Sickles, and Double Hammers, among others. Their characteristics are: the postures are short and simple, the stances sink, and the footwork is stable. They move with unexpected crashing and shaking, and use shouts to carry the qi. They contain many hand techniques and fewer leg techniques, all without embellishment. The spear arts are sturdy and straightforward, using many straight thrusts to the five directions, as well as slipping thrusts; they do not perform flowery movements in the air, but value fighting and actual use, with strong counteroffensive abilities. One example is the Hooked Spear, which was specifically designed to fight against the Jin army's "Heavy-Armored Infantry" and "Cane-Head Cavalry."[44,45]

Biography of Ji Jike 姬際可

(1602–1680) Martial arts practitioner and founder of Xingyi boxing. Courtesy name Longfeng (龍峰, also written 龍鳳). Originally from Puzhou (present-day Yongji County), Hebei Province. According to the preface to Master Li's *Six Harmonies Boxing Manual* (Qing Yongzheng reign period, 1723–1735), the preface to Wang Zicheng's *Queries on the Boxing Treatise,* and section two of the hand-copied *Ji Family Lineage Manual* (*Qianlong* reign period, 1736–1795), Ji Jike was the ninth generation of the Ji family, a family of means, and from an early age he studied literature and martial arts. His skill and bravery were unsurpassed, and he was especially adept in the use of the large spear. Like "a flying horse touching the rafters," he was untouchable after raising his spear and was thus called "Heavenly Spear." In order to adapt to the needs of unarmed self-defense, Jike used the theory of his spear skills as the basis of his theory of boxing, and additionally studied the cleverness of animals' fighting.

He obtained the *Six Harmonies Boxing Classic* by Yue Wumu and researched its concepts diligently for ten years. Using the six harmonies as a methodological base, with the five elements and the ten animals as forms, and considering the mind's causation of movement as intention and the intention's ability as boxing skill, Ji created "the six postures of both front and back." These are the concepts of Xinyi Six Harmonies Boxing: "the mind harmonizes with the intention; the intention harmonizes with the qi; the qi harmonizes with the force; the hands harmonize with the feet; the elbows harmonize with the knees; the shoulders harmonize with the hips." People called this art "Jike Boxing."

According to legend, after his qi was developed, Ji made a visit to the Shaolin Temple at Mt. Song (some say that he resided at the Shaolin Temple for ten years, and there he used the techniques of Shaolin's Five Styles of Boxing to create his art), then passed on his art in Luoyang, Henan Province, and Guichi, Anhui Province. After ten years he returned to his hometown to teach his descendants.

In his later years, Ji defeated roving bandits to the west of his village, killing the bandit leader, and he became known as "Heavenly Spear." He was praised throughout the township, and after his passing, his descendants placed his image in the "Hall of Tribute to Forebears." His disciples are numerous. Wang Yaolong (王耀龍) and Cao Jiwu (曹繼武) are among the most famous.[46]

Biography of Cao Jiwu 曹繼武

(1669–?) One of the principal transmitters of Xingyi boxing. Also called Riwei (日瑋). Originally from Daxing in Zhidai (present-day Beijing), although some sources say he was from Jiyuan County, Henan Province, or from Chizhou (present-day Guichi County), Anhui Province. From an early age, he studied Xingyi and other arts from the art's founder, Ji Jike. However, according to the preface of the *Treatise on Xinyi Six Harmonies Boxing* by Dai Longbang, when Cao Jiwu was living in Qiupu (present-day Guichi County), Anhui Province, he studied Xinyi boxing with a student of Ji Jike's from the south surnamed Zheng.

After twelve years of arduous training, his art was refined and pure, and Cao was both skilled and courageous. In the governmental military tests he was "victorious with three firsts." According to both Zhou Jiannan's *Research on Xingyi Boxing* and the "Martial Worthies" section of the *Guichi County Gazetteer,* Cao Jiwu achieved first place in the Shuntian District examinations in the thirty-second year of the *Kangxi* reign period (1693). The following *Jiaxu* year, at the highest-level military examinations, he graduated first among all candidates; "the Emperor himself selected him as the top grade in the top class, and bestowed upon him the degree of *Jinshi.* "[47] Following this, Cao was made a third-degree imperial Bodyguard, and entered the Forbidden City.

In the thirty-sixth year [1697] he followed the Emperor to attack Elu and, because of his diligent work, was repeatedly called before the court and honored with gifts of clothes, wine, and fruit. In the thirty-ninth year [1700] he was assigned as Adjunct of the Shanxi Province National Guard. Subsequently he received a special commission to become Vice-Commander of the Remote Pacification Guard in Shaanxi Province, and was later promoted to Military Commissioner-in-Chief of Xing'an[48] Regional Command. At this time, there was great flooding on the Han River,[49] and [it is said that] Cao, while directing military troops in round-the-clock relief, suffered hypothermia and died at age thirty-six. Still another story has him retiring later in life and passing on his arts to many disciples in Chizhou and Luoyang.

Dai Longbang (戴龍邦) traveled from Shanxi to Chizhou, where Cao became his teacher. He studied with Cao for ten years, until his art was highly accomplished, and he later became the first generation of the Shanxi branch of Xingyi practitioners. Cao's other outstanding disciple, Ma Xueli (馬學禮), is considered the first generation of the Henan branch of Xingyi practitioners.[50]

Biography of Dai Longbang 戴龍邦

(1713–1802) Founder of the Northern school of Xinyi boxing. Courtesy name Erlei (爾雷). Originally from Qi County, Shanxi Province. From his youth he loved martial arts and studied the Chang-style boxing taught by his family. In the fourth year of the Qing *Yongzheng* reign period (1726) when he was thirteen, Dai Longbang followed his father to Chizhou (present-day Guichi County), Anhui Province, to run a business. There he studied Xinyi Six Harmonies Boxing with Cao Jiwu, and after more than ten years of bitter training attained a deep understanding of its principles.

Dai traveled broadly in Shanxi, Anhui, and Henan provinces, returning to Shanxi in the fifteenth year of the *Qianlong* reign period (1750). While traveling through Luoyang in Henan, he encountered and exchanged ideas with his school brother Ma Xueli, which aided him greatly in further refining his art. With the help of Ma Xueli, Dai wrote the *Treatise on Xinyi Six Harmonies Boxing*. In practice, using the nature of the *tuo* and the *tai*[51] as inspiration, he created the *Tuo* and *Tai* forms, adding these two animal forms to the existing ten forms of Xinyi boxing. Because he considered these to be secret skills, he taught them only to his son Wenliang (文亮) and to his nephews Wenying (文英) and Wenxiong (文雄).[52]

Biography of Li Feiyu 李飛羽

(c. 1809–1890) Martial arts practitioner; the founder of Hebei-style Xingyi boxing. Courtesy name Laoneng (洛能); also called Nengran (能然) or Laonong (老農). Posthumously called Laoneng (老能). Originally from Shen County, Hebei Province. From his youth he was fond of martial arts and first studied Hua-style Boxing.[53] According to "The Inscriptions of Che Yizhai's Tomb," Laoneng once traveled to Taigu in Shanxi Province on business, and it was there he heard that the Dai family of Xiaomu village, Qi County, was skilled in the art of Xinyi boxing. In order to study this art he subsequently moved to Qi County on the pretext of starting a farm and, after a series of unusually clever entreaties and by selecting various people to speak well of him and intercede on his behalf, he finally began studying Xinyi boxing as an official disciple of Dai Wenxiong (courtesy name Erlü) in 1845. At this time Li was already thirty-seven years of age.

After ten years of hard practice and thorough research, he obtained the essential principles of Xinyi boxing. According to Sun Lutang's *True Tales of Boxing Intention,* Laoneng's skill "had reached the highest level." That year Li's sincere friend, an advanced military degree-holder of uncommon strength and skill in fighting arts, was residing in Qi County. One day the two were visiting when the degree-holder unexpectedly grabbed him from behind and tried to pick him up. Laoneng, however, had already jumped up and away from his grasp.

Around the time of the Qing *Xianfeng* reign period (1856), Laoneng was asked to serve as house security for the local wealthy landowner Meng Boru, and it was after this that he began to take disciples. Locals, including Che Yizhai (Yonghong) (車毅齋 (永宏)) and Song Shirong (宋世榮), as well as Liu Qilan (劉奇蘭), Guo Yunshen (郭云深), and Liu Xiaolan (劉曉蘭), all of Hebei Province, were among those who studied his art. In order to spread Xinyi boxing, he combined his own teaching experience with his reorganization of the arts he had learned and thus created something new. From the handwritten version of Li's *Xingyi Boxing Manual,* we can see elements of theory and practice that were not present in the older *Treatise on Xinyi Six Harmonies Boxing* [by Dai Longbang] such as: when training Splitting Fist, he replaced the fist with a palm; in terms of internal skill, he initiated the idea of "three levels of *gongfu*"; and he proposed the idea of "practice to transform essence into qi, practice to transform qi into spirit, and practice to change spirit into nothingness." In addition, Li changed [the character] "Xin" to "Xing" and changed the art's name to Xingyi boxing.

During the process of teaching numerous students, Li gradually formed the idea that, although Xinyi boxing was its origin, Xingyi boxing was a complete and distinct system with its own skills and theory, and he made great contributions to this art. During his life, his students were numerous, and all were outstanding. Aside from those mentioned above, there were Li Jingzhai (李鏡齋), Liu Yuanheng (劉元亨), Zhang Shude (張树德), Bai Xiyuan (白西圜), He Yongheng (贺永恒), Li Guangheng (李廣亨), Li Taihe (李太和), and Liu Zhihe (劉之和), among others. The students of his famous disciples spread throughout China and include Li Cunyi (李存義), Zhang Zhankui (張占魁), Wang Fuyuan (王福元), Wang Kuiyuan (王魁元), Xu Zhan'ao (許占鰲), and Qian Yantang (錢硯堂), among others.[54]

Biography of Guo Yunshen 郭云深

(1820–1901) Famed Xingyi Master. Also called Yusheng (峪生). Originally from Shen County, Hebei Province. Although of short stature, Guo possessed a strong constitution and resolute will. As a youth he enthusiastically studied Shaolin boxing arts, but after practicing for several years had attained little. At the beginning of the Qing *Tongzhi* reign period [1862], he met Li Feiyu, the founder of Hebei-style Xingyi, who explained to him that although the external forms of Xingyi were simple, its theory was profound. Subsequently Guo became Li's student and began studying Xingyi, first studying only *beng quan,* but later learning the complete art. [It is said that] when Li would travel by donkey to other places, Guo would follow behind him practicing *beng quan*. After twelve years of arduous study, Guo had not only fully grasped the principles of applying Xingyi and the mysteries of *ming jin, an jin,* and *hua jin,*[55] but also had attained the essence of broadsword, spear, straight-sword, and staff, and excelled in using *beng quan*. During the third year of the *Guangxu* reign period (1877) Guo began teaching at the Western Tombs, and then became martial arts instructor in the household of the Supervisor-in-Chief of the Six Mausolea, Tan Chongjie. Following this he served as instructor for the Qing Imperial House, teaching Zai Chun and Zai Lian, and later served as adviser to the Prefect of Zhengding Commandery, Qian Xicai, instructing his son Qian Yantang in boxing arts.

Yunshen esteemed chivalry and virtue toward people and detested evil. At the time, the bandit "Local Emperor" Dou Xianjun was harming people in the local villages. Guo killed him in their defense and then turned himself in to authorities. Knowing of Dou's wickedness, the magistrate sentenced Guo to only three years in jail on charges of manslaughter. Because both his feet and hands were shackled and his movement restricted, Guo could practice only "half-step *beng quan*" while jailed. As a result, his art became more supreme, and thus it was said that his "half-step *beng quan* strikes everywhere under Heaven without match." After release from prison, Guo traveled widely throughout northeastern China and Hebei, Shandong, and Henan provinces, all without encountering his equal [in boxing skill]. To test his ability, he would ask five strong young men to each press the points of wooden staffs against his abdomen, which he would then rapidly expand, causing the five men to fly off and land on the ground more than a meter away. It was just as Sun Lutang wrote in his *True Tales of Boxing Intention:* "The principle behind all that Master [Guo] practiced was to make the abdomen completely full, and the mind completely empty. The form and appearance are heavy like Mt. Tai, but the body's movements are lively and nimble like a bird in flight."

Yunshen once traveled to the capital to compare his art with those of the famous Bagua practitioner Dong Haichuan and the famous Taiji practitioner Yang Luchan. Without attempting to determine who was better or worse, they used their martial arts to establish friendship and became the sincerest of friends. Taking the best points and supplementing any shortcomings, they combined and integrated Taiji, Xingyi, and Bagua, and together made great contributions to the development of these arts.

Yunshen was educated in both martial arts and literature, and was also versed in military arts and poetry. He achieved much in his research into the principles and tenets of Xingyi, and in his later years retired to his home-town, where his experiences teaching were set forth in his *Explanation of the Xingyi Boxing Manual.* The students he instructed over the course of his life were quite numerous. Among the most famous are Li Kuiyuan, Qian Yantang, Wang Xiangyuan (王香元), Sun Lutang (孫禄堂), Xu Zhan'ao, and Wang Xiangzhai (王薌齋).[56]

Biography of Liu Qilan 劉奇蘭

(1819–1889) Famed Xingyi practitioner. Originally from Shen County, Hebei Province. From his youth he was fond of the fighting arts and was skilled in many empty-hand and armed arts. He was also very learned and was known as "The Distinguished Gentleman with Sagely Hands." Later he studied Xingyi with Li Feiyu. His attainments were quite profound, and he did not hold to the views of school and style, breaking the traditions of secretiveness and guardedness in teaching. He once raised troops for the gate guard in Shenzhou (present-day Shen County, Hebei Province), then later returned to his hometown.

Qilan was naturally broad-minded, teaching his arts wholeheartedly, and his disciples were as numerous as clouds. Li Cunyi and Zhang Zhankui (among others) are examples of his lineage. Those continuing his art also included his son, Liu Dianchen (劉殿琛), as well as Liu Jintang (劉錦堂), Geng Chengxin (耿成信), Zhou Mingtai (周明泰), Tian Jingjie (田靜傑), Liu Xiaolan,[57] Liu Fengchun (劉鳳春), and Liu Dekuan (劉德寬). Dianchen later wrote *Plucking Out the Subtleties of Xingyi Boxing* to explain and spread his father's theory and art.

Liu Qilan and his school brother Guo Yunshen made a special trip to the capital to call upon Dong Haichuan (董海川) at the residence of Prince Su and to exchange experiences with him. Because both [Guo and Dong] had expertise, they fought for three days without a victor emerging. This led from competition to a mutual admiration and an immediate friendship, and the encounter was spread as a popular story in the martial arts community at the time. After this it was said, "Xingyi and Bagua are united as one school." Thereafter, people also acknowledged the proclamation of the "United Loyalty of the Seven Worthies" or "Sworn Alliance of the Nine Worthies" to "extinguish borders and not divide with limits." The "Seven Worthies" were Liu Qilan's famous disciples Li Cunyi, Zhang Zhankui, Geng Chengxin, Zhou Mingtai, and Liu Dekuan, and Dong Haichuan's famous disciples Cheng Tinghua (程廷華) and Yin Fu (尹福). The "Nine Worthies," aside from the above-mentioned seven people, include Liu Qilan's famous disciples Tian Jingjie and Liu Fengchun.[58]

Biography of Li Cunyi 李存義

(1847–1921) Martial arts practitioner. Originally named Cunyi (存毅), courtesy names Sutang (肅堂) and also Zhongyuan (忠元). Originally from Shen County, Hebei Province. When he was a young man, his family was poor and he made his living in moving services. In his spare time, he practiced various arts and later traveled throughout Shandong, Hebei, and Shanxi searching for teachers. In midlife, he luckily happened upon Liu Qilan and began studying Xingyi boxing and Shaolin-style weapons. Afterward, he studied Xingyi with Guo Yunshen and Bagua with Dong Haichuan. He was also friends with Cheng Tinghua, and he excelled in his study of Bagua, reaching a deep understanding of the art, until Li Cunyi's name was known throughout the country.

In the twentieth year of the Qing *Guangxu* reign period (1894), he accepted a position as a martial arts instructor for the Qing army, later being promoted to Squad Leader under the Superior Security Group of the

Zhejiang and Jiangxi Provinces Commander-in-Chief. Because he had little interest in being a career official, Li gave up his post and moved to Baoding, where he opened the Wantong Bodyguard Service, making his living in the bodyguard profession and teaching many students.

In the twenty-sixth year of the *Guangxu* reign period [1900], the Eight Allied Armies occupied Beijing. In order to resist this foreign insult, Cunyi led his students to join the Boxer Rebellion in the Tianjin area to fight against the invaders. He usually fought at the head of his troops, carrying a single broadsword with which he bravely and fiercely killed many enemies. At the battle of Lao Long Kou in Tianjin, he inflicted heavy casualties on the enemy, and because of this his fame spread greatly and he was nicknamed "Single Saber Li" by his contemporaries. Later, Li gave up the bodyguard trade and concentrated on teaching. His famous students include Shang Yunxiang (尚雲祥), Sun Lutang,[59] Chu Guiting (諸桂亭), Ai Yongchun (艾永春), Huang Bonian (黃柏年), and the "Three Heroes of Dingxing"—Li Caiting (李彩亭),[60] Li Yueting (李躍亭), and Li Wenting (李文亭).

In the third year of the Qing *Xuantong* reign period (1911), in order to inspire the spirit of the masses and to resist the influence of the principles of Japanese *bushido,* Li established—with the help of Ye Yunbiao (葉雲表), Ma Fengtu (馬鳳圖), Li Ruidong (李瑞東), and Zhang Zhankui—the Chinese Martial Artists Assembly. Ye Yunbiao acted as President, and Li acted as Vice-President and Chief Instructor. Among others, they invited the famous teachers Li Shuwen (李書文), Huo Diange (霍殿閣), and Hao Enguang (郝恩光) to be instructors. This Assembly had a considerable influence at the time, and a branch was even established in Japan. Li accepted the invitation of the Generals Wang Zhixiang and Ma Zizhen to serve as Martial Arts Instructor for the Army Corps, and in September 1918, he and Zhang Zhankui led more than ten of his students, including Li Jianqiu (李劍秋) and Han Muxia (韓慕俠), to attend the World Martial Arts Competition in Beijing, where Li Cunyi defeated the arrogant Russian strongman Kangtaier. Later he assumed a position at the Shanghai Jingwu Academy, and also taught at Shanghai Nanyang Public College (the former name of present-day Shanghai Jiaotong University). Following Huo Yuanjia, Li taught Xingyi boxing in Shanghai, and Hebei-style Xingyi boxing flourished in southern China. Li's writings include *A Fighting Arts Instruction Manual, A Compendium of True Xingyi,* and *The Essentials of Northern and Southern Fighting Arts.*[61]

Portrait of Li Cunyi

Biography of Sun Fuquan 孫福全

(1860–1933) Martial arts practitioner. Founder of Sun-Wu-style Taiji,[62] but also skilled in Xingyi and Bagua. Courtesy name Lutang (禄堂); late in life he took the pseudonym Hanzhai (涵斋). Originally from Wan County (present-day Wangdu County), Hebei Province. As a youth he was naturally intelligent and his disposition gentle. He first studied martial arts under Li Kuiyuan, and after several years of focusing primarily on Xingyi boxing had learned all that Li could teach. He continued his studies by obtaining the essence of Xingyi from his Grand-teacher Guo Yunshen, often accompanying Guo in his travels to other provinces, and thus greatly increasing his knowledge and experience. He also received instruction from such elder-generation practitioners as Che Yizhai, Song Shirong, Liu Qilan, and Bai Xiyuan, and thus his Xingyi skill became completely accomplished. Later he traveled to the capital and studied the essentials of Bagua from Cheng Tinghua, fully grasping its mysteries. Because his martial arts skill was deep, he enjoyed the praise of all the capital's [martial arts] masters.

Lutang's appearance was very thin, and his frame small, but his movements were lively and nimble, and so he was called "living monkey Sun Lutang." Later Sun met the famous Taiji practitioner Hao Weizhen (郝維禎), through whose instruction he acquired the subtleties of Wu-style Taiji. In Sun's later years, when his skill had become refined—able to create sublime transformations and adapt his movements to the situation without fixed rules and thus synthesize with thorough comprehension—he combined the essential points of Xingyi, Bagua, and Taiji to create Sun-style Taiji. Lutang read the *Book of Changes* and the *Elixir Classic* and used these to explain boxing theory, establishing the system of thought in martial arts studies that "boxing must be united with the Dao," as well as the principles of "the three fists" uniting as one, and "the pre- and post-Heaven Bagua uniting." The unique characteristics [of Sun-style Taiji] include "advancing and retreating follow one another, one must have a root when stepping and pull back when retreating"; "movements should be relaxed, open, and lively, and one's agility natural"; "in practice one must clearly differentiate solid and empty in the two feet, continuously without cease like floating clouds or running water"; and "when changing direction, one should always use both 'opening' and 'closing' to meet." Thus this art was also called "Opening and Closing Lively-Step Taiji Boxing." The Xingyi that Sun taught also contained some of the essence of both Bagua and Taiji.

Between 1915 and 1925, Sun secluded himself away to research and to concentrate on writing, producing five specialized works in all: *The Study of Form-Intention Boxing; The Study of Eight Diagrams Palm; The Study of Supreme Ultimate Boxing; The Study of Eight-Diagrams Broadsword;* and *True Tales of Boxing Intention.* His writings were rich, and started the flow of martial arts–specialized writing. Lutang's martial arts virtue was lofty and his martial arts skill unsurpassed. Although he was not once defeated during his lifetime of comparing skills with others, he was never conceited and always emphasized that "the purpose of cultivating martial arts is to develop one's disposition."

At the end of the Qing Dynasty, at the request of Xu Shichang,[63] Sun became an Internal Investigator in Fengtian, where he later was promoted to District Magistrate. In 1918, he served as Vice-Commandant in the Presidential Office, then subsequently was made a Commissioner, and later accepted a post as a Major in the army. In 1928, he accepted an appointment as Wudang-Arts Bureau Chief at the Central Martial Arts Academy, and later served simultaneously as the Vice-Director and Head of Instructional Affairs for the Jiangsu Province National Arts Academy. Late in life he returned to his hometown, and passed away without sickness. His students are numerous, and among the most famous are his disciples Sun Jianyun (孫劍雲), Sun Cunzhou (孫存周), Qi Gongbo (齊公博), Sun Zhenchuan (孫振川), Sun Zhendai (孫振岱), and Hu Fengshan (胡風山).[64]

Portrait of Sun Fuquan

Biography of Shang Yunxiang 尚雲祥

(1864–1937) Famed Xingyi practitioner. Courtesy name Jiting (霽庭) or, in some sources, Jiting (集亭). Originally from Leling County, Shandong Province. As a youth, he traveled with his father to do business in Beijing, where he developed an interest in martial arts. He first studied Gongli boxing[65] from Ma Dayi. Once, when testing his skills, he was defeated by the Xingyi boxing practitioner Li Zhihe (李志和)[66] and realized that Xingyi boxing was an exceptional art. Thereupon he became a disciple of Li Cunyi and practiced Xingyi boxing diligently.

After his art was skillful, he took a position as Inspector with the military body of the five cities, and later served as Head of House Security for the Qing Court Eunuch and Area Military Commander-in-Chief Li. Because his Xingyi skills were outstanding, Shang aroused the interest of Guo Yunshen, from whom he received secret teachings, and his skills became even more refined, especially his foot skill, which earned him the nickname "Iron-leg Buddha." He also learned the essence of Guo Yunshen's *beng quan* and became skilled in this as well. After studying with Guo Yunshen, Shang was also nicknamed [as was Guo himself] by many as "the one whose half-step *beng quan* strikes everywhere under Heaven." Shang once used the *Tai* form to defeat Miyun County's "Spirit Sand Palm" Feng Luozheng. Shang used "split grab connect wrap capture" to defeat a spear-stab toward his throat by big-spear practitioner Ma Xiu from Shunyi County, also known as the "Iron Arhat" of Henan Province. He soundly defeated and assisted authorities in the capture of the great thief of Tongzhou, "Big Boss Eighth Kang" Kang Tianxin, a skilled fighter versed in lightness skill who had harmed many in the area. After this, Shang Yunxiang's fame spread throughout China. His disciples include Jin Yunting, Zhao Keli (趙克禮), Sun Mengzhi (孫夢之), Xu Yuzhi (許羽之), and Li Wenbin (李文彬).[67]

Portrait of Shang Yunxiang

Biography of Jin Yunting 靳雲亭

Master Zhenqi, courtesy name Yunting, is a person of Wuqiao, Hebei Province. His father Huatang practiced boxing outside of work, and at age seven Master studied it as sport, and could mimic just like an adult, but subsequently stopped due to many illnesses. At age twelve he arrived at the capital, where he associated with the two masters Zhao Keli (趙克禮) and Li Lan (李兰), and first began studying Xingyiquan. This boxing is divided into five postures, called Splitting, Smashing, Drilling, Pounding, and Crossing; they possess the blending of hard and soft, and the subtlety of the mutual creation of the five elements. At the time, Masters Shang Yunxiang and Sun Lutang used their boxing to instruct disciples, and Master Jin entered into their schools. Aside from Xingyiquan, he simultaneously studied Taiji and other arts, and with a singular will and determined heart researched and practiced for ten years. During this time he also received Li Cunyi's secret instruction, which advanced his learning, solidified his strength, and made famous his reputation. During the first year of the republic, commander of the infantry Jiang Chaozong (江朝宗)[68] engaged him to instruct the capital commandery. Xiang Cheng[69] heard of his reputation and invited him to supervise and instruct his childern. After Xiang Cheng died, his son Keding recommended that Jin go to a certain official in Baoding but, because Master despised this person, he did not go, and thereafter entered into the technical school of the *Yude* School[70] as a teacher while simultaneously serving as martial arts instructor for the fifteen military divisions at Nanyuan. Because of this, his art flourished among the people of the north. Seeing the changing political situation, the corruption of the military, and recognizing the coming chaos, Master escaped to the south one year, residing in Piling[71] with the Sheng family, who treated him as an esteemed guest and whose sons received his instruction. Those in Shanghai of brave bearing who esteemed boxing presented gifts and sought instruction until his doorsteps were thronged, and Master was forced to select those to admit, not squandering his teachings on the rash or corrupt. Those he viewed as friends, including Sheng Yulin, Lü Zibin, and Wu Dicheng, all gained access to Master's school, and were all cautious and prudent, with the airs of gentlemen. When [Wang Wen] Ru (王文濡)[72] met Master through Mr. Wu's introduction, he was already bothered by sickness of the limbs and was lame, making walking awkward. However, because Master explained that Xingyiquan could end illness and encouraged him to undertake study, he trained irregularly—sometimes in the morning or sometimes at nighttime—for five years. Although his illness had not completely gone, his four limbs felt relatively energetic and powerful. When he could walk along with the trolleys or climb through tall grass without falling, he could see Master's excellent skill in gradually leading others. Master's appearance was handsome and strong, his mind gentle. He conducted himself as a teacher with respect, and made friends with sincerity. In regards to weapons, he became adept at one after another, and was especially skilled in straight-sword arts. Although he had not studied much, he was restrained and adaptable, with righteousness his main tenet; this was one reason for his refusal to the certain official. After the capital Martial Arts Institute was established, [Sun] Lutang summoned him to work there; however, Master viewed his own art as only a minor achievement, and the risk of jealousy too great, and so gracefully declined. That year in summer, when the Shanghai Volunteer Corps began traveling performances and took the stage in the Gu Family Courtyard to show their skill, the applause was thunderous, but Master still regarded this self-promotion as shameful, and from this Ru knew Master was a centered and courteous person, and could not be compared to one of those bravos who count on their prowess, self-aggrandizing while insulting others. Ru feigns shame at a lack of letters and the inability to commend him in some small part, but endeavored in his responsibility to pass on this small unofficial biography. As Wang Wenru said of Master Jin:

> Master's teaching was rational, taking my weakened body
> and stiff limbs and patiently correcting them, without forcing

or exhausting, slowly and imperceptibly changing my fearful and complacent heart, attaining the eradication of sickness and extending of life, leading me to today become a teacher. To be able to do this, are these achievements not worth recognizing? As to his conduct, in friendship he was superior, with penetrating purity, unyielding force, and disdain for fame and fortune. All those so-called great men and idealists today, do they possess these qualities? Master Han Fei said: "The literati by means of letters disturbed laws, the cavaliers by means of weapons transgressed prohibitions."[73] Now literati who have disturbed the laws I have already seen numerous times, but as to cavaliers transgressing prohibitions, when I am with Master I cannot fully believe the words of this text.

BIBLIOGRAPHY

Han Fei. *The Complete Works of Han Fei Tzu: A Classic of Chinese Legalism,* 2 vols. Translated by W. K. Liao. London: Probsthain, 1939. Retrieved 11/25/2013 from www2.iath.virginia.edu/saxon/servlet/SaxonServlet?source=xwomen /texts/hanfei.xml&style=xwomen/xsl/dynaxml.xsl&chunk.id=d2.49&toc .depth=1&toc.id=0&doc.lang=bilingual.

Hucker, Charles O. A Dictionary of Official Titles in Imperial China. Stanford, CA: Stanford University Press, 1985.

Jiang Jinshi (江金石). *Xingyi Quan Rumen* (形意拳入門). Tainan, Taiwan: Xinhong Chubanshe (信宏出版社), 1999.

Knoblock, John. *Xunzi: A Translation and Study of the Complete Works.* Vol. 2. Stanford, CA: Stanford University Press, 1988.

Li Jianqiu. *The Art of Xingyiquan* (形意拳術). Taiyuan: Shanxi Science and Technology Publishing House, 2001.

Li Jianqiu. *The Art of Xingyiquan by Li Jianqiu [1920].* Translated by Paul Brennann. Retrieved 5/2013 from http://brennantranslation.wordpress.com/.

Liang Shou-Yu, and Jwing-Ming Yang. *Xingyiquan: Theory, Applications, Fighting Tactics and Spirit.* Boston: YMAA Publication Center, 2002.

Maciocia, Giovanni. *The Foundations of Chinese Medicine.* London: Churchill Livingstone, 1989.

McNeil, James W. *Hsing-I.* Burbank, CA: Unique Publications.

Miller, Dan, ed. *Pa Kua Chang Journal* 4, no. 3 (1994).

Miller, Dan, and Tim Cartmell. *Xing Yi Nei Gong: Xing Yi Health Maintenance and Internal Strength Development.* Pacific Grove, CA: High View Publications, 1994.

Muller, Charles, ed. Digital Dictionary of Buddhism. Retrieved 4/22/2003 from the DDB website: www.acmuller.net/ddb/index.html.

Muller, Charles. *Mencius (Selections).* Retrieved 4/22/2003 from the Resources for East Asian Language and Thought website: www.human.toyogakuen-u .ac.jp/~acmuller/contao/mencius.htm.

Rickett, W. Allyn. *Guanzi: Political, Economic, and Philosophical Essays From Early*

China: A Study and Translation. Princeton, NJ: Princeton University Press, 1985.

Sun Lutang. *Xing Yi Quan Xue: The Study of Form-Mind Boxing.* Translated by Albert Liu, edited by Dan Miller. Pacific Grove, CA: High View Publications, 1993.

Sun Wu. *Sun Tzu's The Art of War.* Translated by Lionel Giles. El Paso, TX: El Paso Norte Press, 2009.

Xue Dian (薛顛). *Xingyi Quanshu Jiang Yi* (形意拳術講義). Taibei, Taiwan: Yiwen Chubanshe (逸文出版社), 2000.

Zhang Shan (張山), ed. *Zhongguo Wushu Baike Quanshu* (中國武術百科全書). Beijing: Zhongguo Baike Quanshu Chubanshe (中國百科全書出版社), 1998.

Essential Teachings on Yue Wumu's Xingyiquan. n.d.

Retrieved 10/2013 from http://blog.sina.com.cn/s/blog_69265c790102dx9s .html.

Retrieved 10/2013 from http://wenku.baidu.com /view/23692afbfab069dc5022010d.html.

Retrieved 10/2013 from http://ishare.iask.sina.com.cn/download/explain .php?fileid=19921128.

Retrieved 10/2013 from www.wushuweb.com/x1/portal.php?mod=view&aid=85.

NOTES

1. 宮保, an honorary government title under the Qing Dynasty. Here Minister of Transportation Sheng Xuanhuai.
2. The posthumous title of the Song Dynasty general Yue Fei.
3. 五行拳, usually rendered as Five Element Boxing. Though there is considerable linguistic and historical argument for translating 五行 as "Five Phases," "Five Transformations," "Five Actions," or similarly, I have retained the more commonly known "Five Elements" throughout the text.
4. 元氣, original or congenital *qi*.
5. Pen name of Ling Guiqing (凌桂青).
6. *Mengzi*, Book 2, part I, chapter 2, section 9. As Charles Muller writes:

> The Chinese ideograph *ch'i* originally means "air," especially breath. Through Mencius' usage, and the usage of later Taoists, martial artists, and the Neo-Confucian school, its meaning becomes quite enhanced. Here *ch'i*, as breath, is understood as the vital connection between body and mind. It is the life-force which animates the body to greater or lesser degrees, depending upon its cultivation toward the vigor and vitality of the individual. In the terms with which Mencius describes it, *ch'i* can be compared to the *prana* of some Indian yogic systems, which can be cultivated through breath control and various other yogic practices.
>
> One of the most relevant points that Mencius makes in regard to the cultivation of *ch'i* is that this cultivation is dependent, more than anything else, on the uninterrupted practice of Righteousness.

Muller's translation of sections 9–16 is as follows:

> Ch'ou asked, "Will you please tell me about your 'mental stability' in relation to Kao Tzu's 'mental stability'?"
>
> Mencius replied, "Kao Tzu says that what cannot be attained through words should not be sought for in the mind, and that what cannot be attained in the mind should not be sought for through the *ch'i*. This latter proposition is correct, but the first one is not. The *will*

is the director of the *ch'i,* and the *ch'i* is something that permeates the body. So the will is primary and the *ch'i* is secondary. Therefore, it is said: 'Hold on to your will; do not scatter your *ch'i.'*"

Ch'ou said, "You just said that the will is primary; and the *ch'i* is secondary. Now you say, 'hold on to your will; don't scatter your *ch'i.'* Why do you say this?"

Mencius said, "The will influences the *ch'i* and the *ch'i* influences the will. For instance, jumping and running, though most directly concerned with the *ch'i,* also have an effect on the mind."

"May I ask in what it is that you are superior?"

"I understand language, and I am good at nourishing my vast *ch'i.*"

"What do you mean by 'vast *ch'i*'?"

"That is difficult to explain. *Ch'i* can be developed to great levels of quantity and stability by correctly nourishing it and not damaging it, to the extent that it fills the space between Heaven and Earth. In developing *ch'i,* if you are connected with Righteousness and the Tao, you will never be in want of it. It is something that is produced by accumulating Righteousness, and is not something that you can grab from superficial attempts at Righteousness. If you act without mental composure, you will become *ch'i*-starved.

"Therefore I would say that Kao Tzu has not yet understood Righteousness, since he regards it as something external. You must be willing to work at it, understanding that you cannot have precise control over it. You can't forget about it, but you can't force it to grow, either.

"You don't want to be like the man from Sung. There was a man from Sung who was worried about the slow growth of his crops and so he went and yanked on them to accelerate their growth. Empty-headed, he returned home and announced to his people: 'I am so tired today. I have been out stretching the crops.' His son ran out to look, but the crops had already withered. Those in the world who don't 'help their crops by pulling' are few indeed. There are also those who regard all effort as wasteful and don't even weed their crops. But those who think they can hurry their growth along by forcing it are not only not helping their *ch'i,* but actually harming it!"

7. *Mengzi,* Book 2, part I, chapter 2, section 11.

8. As noted in the *Digital Dictionary of Buddhism,* www.acmuller.net/ddb/index. html, the *Mahāprajñāpāramitā-sūtra* (般若波羅蜜多經), the Wisdom Sutra, is a general term for the sutras that teach the perfection of wisdom, i.e., emptiness (空). This most likely refers to the *Heart of Wisdom Sutra,* a widely known and commonly chanted Buddhist text whose core tenet is that "emptiness is form, and form is emptiness."

9. The clear and turbid fluids. For a detailed discussion, see Giovanni Maciocia, *The Foundations of Chinese Medicine.* London: Churchill Livingstone, 1989, p. 35.

10. The text of the 1930 edition follows the common creative sequence order—Pi, Zuan, Beng, Pao, and Heng. The 1931 edition lists the elements in the "central harmony" sequence—Pi, Beng, Zuan, Pao, and Heng.

11. Both the 1930 and 1931 editions use 中腕 for 中脘, "Central Venter" (REN-12).

12. Ji Shou is usually listed as Ji Jike's son, not Cao's student. Ma Xueli is usually listed as a school brother of Dai Longbang, not his teacher, and Dai is listed as a direct student of Cao.

13. Rickett, W. Allyn. *Guanzi: Political, Economic, and Philosophical Essays from Early China: A Study and Translation.* Princeton, NJ: Princeton University Press, 1985. Vol. 1, p. 333.

14. Knoblock, John. *Xunzi: A Translation and Study of the Complete Works.* Stanford, CA: Stanford University Press, 1988. Vol. 2, p. 222.

15. My translation.

16. See note 12.

17. Li Nengran, or Li Laoneng: the characters "ran" or "Lao" were for some reason omitted.

18. The space that is three *cun* behind the center of the eyebrows.

19. The Chinese inch, traditionally measured as the width of a person's thumb at the knuckle.

20. Neither of these two sequences shows up again in either edition, and no note is made of their significance.

21. There are many variations of this text; however, the earliest versions of it seem to appear in this text and in *The Art of Xingyiquan* by Li Jianqiu. For an

alternate translation of the nine teachings, see the Li version translation by Paul Brennan.

22. If viewed facing the person.

23. Possibly the twelve back *shu* points (UB-13, 14, 15, 18, 19, 20, 21, 22, 23, 25, 27, and 28) directly associated with the organs, plus the *qihai* and *guanyuan* points (UB-24 and UB-26).

24. The hair of the head and of the body.

25. 天庭 "Heavenly Palace": the center of the forehead.

26. 印堂 "Hall of the Seal" (M-HN-3).

27. 承漿 "Sauce Receptacle" (REN-24).

28. 涌泉 "Bubbling Well" (KI-1).

29. The original text has first-person "me," which seems incongruous.

30. The text after this point was probably originally a separate section.

31. This section seems to have been a later addition, and is interspersed with numerous incorrectly written characters that change the meaning of the text. This translation tries to interpolate based on several versions of the text and referring to textual analysis available online.

32. Here "scissor legs" refers to the shearing action of the legs in stepping forward. This same term is also used to mean a slightly forward-weighted twisted horse stance as in note 38 below.

33. Paraphrasing the *Art of War*. Translation by Giles.

34. The three processes of transforming the bones, transforming the tendons, and washing the marrow.

35. 人, a description of the position of the feet. Usually seen in Xingyi texts as "*ba-shape feet*" (八字形).

36. There is some discussion as to the exact anatomical meaning of *kua*. Generally, it can be thought of as the inguinal crease externally and the lateral rotator group internally.

37. The eye of the fist.

38. A slightly forward-weighted twisted horse stance.

39. 十字步, also called 剪步. A step through with a following step.

40. Although the same phrase as described in note 32, here it denotes the movement of the legs as they come together.

41. These rhymes appear in both the 1930 and 1931 editions as seven words with three important didactic phrases. Although both editions have the same seven words, some phrases are longer in the 1930 version, and sometimes the two versions have completely different phrases. Here I have taken the longer of any duplicate phrases, and included each unique item from the two editions, in some cases resulting in more than three important points.

42. During the Song Dynasty, one *jin* was equal to 633 grams—thus, a 418-pound bow.

43. During the Song Dynasty, one *dan* was equal to 75.96 kilograms—thus, a 1,337-pound crossbow.

44. A military formation with two wings of skilled cavalry facing in at the sides of the main infantry, looking like the heads of two canes.

45. *Zhongguo Wushu Baike Quanshu,* edited by Shan Zhang (Beijing: Zhongguo Baike Quanshu Chubanshe, 1998), pp. 531–532.

46. *Zhongguo Wushu Baike Quanshu,* p. 538.

47. "Advanced Gentleman," the highest rank under the old examination system.

48. A city in northeast Jiangxi Province.

49. A tributary of the Yangtze River in Shanxi Province.

50. *Zhongguo Wushu Baike Quanshu,* p. 541.

51. 鼍, alligator, and 鳥台 , the *tai* bird, a Saker falcon, commonly translated as phoenix.

52. *Zhongguo Wushu Baike Quanshu,* pp. 542–543.

53. 花拳

54. *Zhongguo Wushu Baike Quanshu,* pp. 544–545.

55. 明勁, 暗勁, 化勁， The three principles of internal power.

56. *Zhongguo Wushu Baike Quanshu,* p. 547.

57. A probable error. Liu Xiaolan was Liu Qilan's school brother, not student, and no other sources list a student by that name.

58. *Zhongguo Wushu Baike Quanshu,* pp. 546–547.

59. Though Sun Lutang studied widely with many prominent martial artists, most biographies do not list Li Cunyi as one of his teachers.

60. Most sources list Li Haiting (李海亭).

61. *Zhongguo Wushu Baike Quanshu,* p. 548.

62. 孫武太極拳

63. A prominent Qing Dynasty official and, later, political reformer under the Republican government.

64. *Zhongguo Wushu Baike Quanshu,* p. 550.

65. 功力拳

66. Li Zhihe's name does not appear on any of the common lineage charts, though he is presumably a student of Li Cunyi.

67. *Zhongguo Wushu Baike Quanshu,* p. 550.

68. Jiang Chaozong (江朝宗) was Chinese General, Chief of the Beijing Commandery, and acting Premier of the Republic of China in 1917.

69. It is not clear to whom this refers.

70. Possibly Baoding Yu De College (保定育德中学).

71. Present-day Changzhou.

72. The text states only "Ru (濡)" but shortly afterward quotes Wang Wenru (王文濡). This is possibly the same Wang Wenru who was editor for the Zhonghua Book Company and Shanghai Commercial Press.

73. 儒以文亂法，俠以武犯禁. Translation by Wenkui Liao.

ABOUT THE TRANSLATOR

JOHN GROSCHWITZ IS CURRENTLY an Instructor in Shen Long Xingyi and Cheng School Gao Style Bagua with the North American Tang Shou Tao Association. He has also studied Liang Zhenpu Bagua, Song Shirong Xingyi, Kajukenbo, Northern Shaolin, Lanshou Quan, Water Boxing, Yang and Wu-Hao Taiji, and various systems of Qi Gong, in the U.S. and Mainland China.

John has studied Chinese language and literature for more than twenty years and has worked as a translator, interpreter, and lecturer. He graduated with B.A. degrees in Chinese and Art Practice from the University of California, Berkeley, and with an M.A. in East Asian Studies from Stanford University. Most recently he translated the *Cheng School Gao Style Baguazhang Manual*.